Wakefield Press

# Prospect Hill: Memories of a Burned Village

# Prospect Hill:
## Memories of a Burned Village

Claire Smith, Heather Burke, Jordan Ralph,
George Merryman, Jo Smith and the
Prospect Hill Community

with photographs by Jiayuan Liang

Wakefield
Press

Wakefield Press
16 Rose Street
Mile End
South Australia 5031
www.wakefieldpress.com.au

First published 2021



Cover design by Liz Nicholson, Wakefield Press
Typeset by Michael Deves, Wakefield Press

ISBN 978 1 74305 835 0

A catalogue record for this book is available from the National Library of Australia

*This book is dedicated to*

KEITH JOHN GRIGGS

# Contents

# Foreword

History gets lost too quickly. People today are not really aware of Aboriginal cultural burning traditions so that information is not factored into fire management plans. My own learning experiences in this regard was when a group of Aboriginal people who lived just outside of Yalata in what was called the 20-mile camp, to Oak Valley, near Maralinga. They set up a community there. When I first went there representing the Aboriginal and Torres Strait Islander Commission (ATSIC) all they had was a water tank. When I saw how they looked after the land it made me aware that Aboriginal people had detailed knowledge of how to control growth. I became more aware of the need for Aboriginal people with knowledge to work to prevent some of the real disasters that Australia experiences in terms of bushfires. That said, I notice that the government recently set up a special committee on bushfire management that included Indigenous Australians, with the aim of working together to prevent such disasters. I am hopeful there will be progress. There are basic concepts that need to be widely understood. On Ngadjuri lands I notice that even today people put their crops right up against the fence – there is no fire break. My wife Brenda's father had a property, and we always had a fire break. Small country towns, areas that get plenty of rain and plenty of growth, need to have a three-mile firebreak. There has to be a sizable break. Otherwise, you don't have any control. The fire is going to control you.

History is important to Aboriginal people. We need to have an Aboriginal history for every region of Australia. For a long time I have been concerned about the absence of Aboriginal histories across Australia. Aboriginal people lived across the country, and every region has its own Aboriginal histories. We have done what we can in Ngadjuri lands but there is still much more work to be done. I call on academics across Australia to work with Aboriginal people to research Aboriginal histories. Most importantly, I call on scholars to train Aboriginal people to research their own histories. Aboriginal people have their own interests and they will direct research into areas that non-Aboriginal people might well overlook. This will build a rich, new body of work – Aboriginal histories written by Aboriginal people. Moreover, research training and experience will increase skills and build capacity in Aboriginal communities. This will help to Close the Gap in education, employment, health – and lifespan. Research skills make Aboriginal people better placed to get employment in government or business, or as consultants. Given an opportunity, some Aboriginal people will choose an academic pathway themselves.

*Prospect Hill: Memories of a Burned Village* is a book about ordinary people living ordinary lives, at times in extraordinary circumstances. The Ash Wednesday bushfires set the scene for these people to pull from themselves the strength they needed to confront those fires. It tells the stories of Prospect Hill, a small community in rural South Australia. Sometimes the stories are of endurance, capturing the strength and resilience of rural populations. Sometimes they reveal a kind of everyday heroism as people deal with the routine challenges of lives that were lived in sometimes harsh conditions. Some aspects of the stories are mundane. These parts are also important as the mundane details of life are rarely captured in government records or newspaper articles, or even in letters.

Reading the stories in this book was a bit like reading my own history. In my 17 years at Curramulka, we felt the same. We were always concerned about the fires. The community did exactly what the Prospect Hill community did, getting a fire truck and equipment. In the future, it seems that fires are going to be fought more from the air. If it stops the fires, that is what people are looking for. Prospect Hill is typical of many rural towns in Australia, as bushfires are part of a pattern of life in rural Australia. However, the intensity of these fires is changing, and the frequency of major bushfire disasters seem to be increasing. This could be related to climate change. I've noticed that the seasons are changing, getting longer or shorter. In some areas in the past, you could bank on the rain coming on Anzac Day every year. The farmer would plan to start to plough their field around this time. All of a sudden, it doesn't rain until a week later, and this changes the timing of when you plant the seed. It plays a big part. As a country, we need to monitor climate change and work to better understand its effects.

I was very happy to write the Foreword for this book. Since 1998, I have worked closely with Claire Smith and her husband, anthropologist Gary Jackson, recording sites on Ngadjuri lands. This has been a long and fruitful collaboration. This book is an outcome of the community archaeology program at Flinders University. It is part of a movement within universities that seeks to undertake research that is of value to communities, that engages with the challenges that are faced by societies and that has social impact. This is a book about a small community, but it has a big impact in recording stories that might otherwise be lost. It is a book, not a digital product. It is something you can hold in your hand, give to a family member. You can read it even if you do not own a computer. It is my pleasure to endorse this book.

Vincent Copley senior AO, 22 October 2020

# One Little Spot That Didn't Burn

My cows had all run into a corner of a paddock, up a bit of a hill by a dam over there. There was no way they'd get out ... I had my little dog in the car and I was looking after a sick dog of my Auntie's ... and my pet possum ... the little dogs were terrified when the fire come all around ... The flames was about eight foot high, just going across this paddock. I got across there in my vehicle – my car with my dogs and the possum in it. ... I called [the cows] and they started running down this hill where the flames were – running through the flames to me. I'll never forget the sight: they were holding their heads right up in the air, keeping their eyes and their mouths – trying to – [keep] out of the flames. And of course their tails. They got their hair burnt off their tails. ... Oh, but then they milled around me. They stayed all around this one little spot. I was just in the one little spot that didn't burn. There was two little calves let out ... [that] I was feeding by hand. ... I thought, 'Oh, that's the finish of those.' A while later ... It ... went pitch black when the fire was all around. You couldn't see, you couldn't breathe. It was terrible. And I felt something hit me in the back of the legs. And I put my hand down, and there – these two little calves. They'd come down 'round the edge of the fire, and they'd found me. Way down by the part of the property where I was with the cows. And they found me. They were sort of snuggled in against my legs ... And they stuck there by me. Some of the cows would go to walk away, and I'd call their name – because they all had names – and they'd all rush back ... And there was this great big old six-foot kangaroo there amongst us. And this bull that I'd bought, that I hadn't see for two days, he arrived there, too. From then on, we got on very well together ... I saved all my animals, thank goodness ... Was weeks and weeks and weeks treating them with cream, bringing them in every day ... I'll never, ever forget that day. I said, somebody was with me that day. That's for sure. I was very lucky. On seventy-two acres, I was in the one little spot that didn't burn.

Joyce Smart, 12 March 2014

# Preface

This book was written at the request of the Prospect Hill Community Association. It emerges from an oral history project that was launched after Ray Bailey of the Prospect Hill community approached Heather Burke of Flinders University. Heather put Ray in contact with Claire Smith and the Flinders University Archaeological Society, who agreed to help locate artefacts at a surveyor's camp dating from the initial settlement of Prospect Hill. Oral histories hold that a location named 'Survey Hill', near Prospect Hill, was the location of this camp. Members of the Flinders University Archaeological Society conducted fieldwork at Survey Hill and, although a number of items were recorded, including glass and ceramic fragments and children's figurines, the materials were relatively recent. No trace of a nineteenth-century surveyor's camp was found.

While the archaeological survey did not continue, Jordan Ralph, in his capacity as President of the Flinders University Archaeological Society, continued working with the community. Together with Greg Morrison, Chair of the Prospect Hill Community Association, Jordan developed an oral history project that recorded the stories of older people from the community, many of whom hold an archive of heritage stories that have not previously been documented in any way. The contributors to this book were selected by the Prospect Hill Community

Association for their knowledge and attachment to the town. As befits a group of people focused on sharing the history of their community to visitors and locals alike, many are avid storytellers and the immense pride they display in the history of their town is a remarkable, contagious part of their anecdotes. Deane Michelmore, Joyce Smart, Pat Connor and Ray Bailey were approached because of their intimate knowledge of the history of Prospect Hill and their long-term association with the community. Jack Lovelock was approached as one of the last remaining dairy farmers, and Brenda Nisbett as someone who had lived her formative years in the community working in the local post office. Glenys and Graeme Usher were closely involved with the Blackfellows Creek Country Fire Service at the time of the 1983 Ash Wednesday fires. All interviewees were provided with a list of standardised questions well ahead of the recording sessions, which, while certainly helping them to prepare their answers, may also have curtailed the stories they might otherwise have told naturally or candidly. Many people recreated their own versions of the area's core stories – an interesting result in itself – which shows that some stories have greater resonance in establishing and reinforcing community identities. Some of these tales include how Prospect Hill and Blackfellows Creek were named, the story of the ill-fated trek taken by Sarah McHarg on 3rd June 1841, in the very early days of European settlement, and the ways in which a handful of families helped to shape the historical and contemporary community.

The knowledge contained in these stories is both rich and precarious. When we started this project, we understood that if these stories were not recorded soon they would be lost. Since then, two of the eight people who were interviewed, Pat Connor and Joyce Smart, have passed away. The interviews that make up this book were undertaken jointly by Jordan Ralph and Antoinette Hennessy. Dianne Riley helped with the transcriptions. In their chapter forms, each interview has been edited for length and clarity, though we have tried to retain the flavour of the language. Transcripts of the full, unedited interviews are available on the website that complements this book, *Sharing the Heritage of Prospect Hill* (https://prospecthillheritage.com/).

A major challenge when compiling this book was to ensure that it did not contribute to an erasure of Aboriginal people. While Prospect Hill is located on the lands of the Peramangk Aboriginal people, there are no Peramangk people living in the community at this time, nor were they there at the time of Ash Wednesday. This posed a serious dilemma. All of Australia is Aboriginal land. Writing any history of rural Australia (or any part of Australia) without including Aboriginal voices contributes to an erasure of Aboriginal people from the histories of their lands. We addressed this challenge by calling on two eminent Aboriginal people. We reproduce a brief outline of the history and culture of the Peramangk people, written by Peramangk Elder, Ivan Copley AO. In addition, Ngadjuri Elder, Vince Copley senior AO, has kindly written the foreword for this book. We are grateful to both of them.

We thank Michael Bollen from Wakefield Press for taking on this publication and helping to shape its final form. Antoinette Hennessy filmed the interviews undertaken by Jordan Ralph and took most of the photographs of people who were interviewed. She also assisted with developing the website, *Sharing the Heritage of Prospect Hill*. Antoinette Hennessy, Matthew Ebbs and Jiayuan Liang assisted with archival research and Jiayuan Liang took the contemporary photographs that appear throughout. Fiona Brady drew the map in Figure 3. Gary Jackson and Paulyn Kerr kindly assisted with proof-reading the text. Greg Morrison was our point

Figure 1. Claire Smith discussing this book at Prospect Hill Community Association Meeting, 13 October, 2020. Photo: Jiayuan Liang.

person with the Prospect Hill community and Gail Morrison kindly hosted our visits to the museum. Glenys and Graeme Usher kindly provided archival photographs from their family collection. We also thank the Bailey and the Gibson families for photographs. On a visit to South Australia, Professor Marius-Tiberiu Alexianu of Universitatea Alexandru Ioan Cuza in Iasi, Romania, suggested the title for this book. This research was funded by the Federal Department of Sustainability, Environment, Water, Population and Communities. The Prospect Hill Community Association provided funds to allow the production of colour photos. Figures 6, 14, 15, 30 and 39 are provided courtesy of the State Library of South Australia. The second image in Figure 14 is courtesy of the History Trust of South Australia. Figure 2, the photograph of the painting 'Black Thursday, February 6, 1851', by William Strutt, 1864, is published courtesy of the State Library of Victoria. We thank Lyn Williams and the Williams family for allowing us to use the image of Fred Williams' painting 'After Bushfire 1' (1968).

# Story of the Peramangk People

## Ivan Copley AO

Peramangk Peoples (known as the 'Fire Makers' and also 'Red Ochre Peoples'), because of their use and access to Red Ochre, flint and mineral pyrites, lived on the eastern side of the escarpment of the Mount Lofty Ranges. Records indicate approximately 600 Peramangk living around Mount Barker and at least 1,200 across its Nation and Claim areas at the time of European colonisation.

There are still many descendants living today in South Australia. The whole language of these people has not survived, but there are still many words, including the names of places and names of the Clans that made up the Peramangk Nation.

The Peramangk people share close relationships, culture and some language with the Nations of the Kaurna to the west, Ngadjuri to the north, Ngarrindjeri to the south and Meru to the east. The Peramangk lived in the strip of country running north from Mount Barker through Harrogate, Gumeracha, Mount Pleasant and Springton, to the Angaston district and south to Strathalbyn. There are also sites along the River Murray where Peramangk people had access to the River, Peramangk place names can still be found at these places. Peramangk people had relations along the River Murray, Mannum and areas north of Manunka and around it to Swan Reach.

The Peramangk Clan Group of Mertingeragal includes the areas around Mount Barker, the Mount Barker Summit, Brukunga, Native Valley and Harrogate up to the back of Mount Torrens and across to Kanmantoo. This is the land of my Father, his Father and our ancestors. The Summit and the smaller hill next to it, where Ngeringa Cultural Centre now sits, were both used by the Ngarrindjeri nation.

The smaller hill was very significant for funeral Ceremonies and artworks kept at the Adelaide Museum capture the Smoking Ceremonies that were performed there by the Ngarrindjeri Peoples. It is still a significant place of importance.

There was trading between the Peramangk and the Aboriginal people in adjoining Nations, with them supplying ochre, flint, quartz, supple whip-stick mallee spears, opossum skins and other items not found on the plains and lower lakes. They would remain at the campsite for several days before moving to prevent overuse of the area and its food supply/resources, thus ensuring the environment stayed the same for future generations over thousands of years.

The Peramangk would return to the sites used in previous years depending on the seasons and the condition of the environment. The diet also varied according to the season, with vegetables, seeds, honey, eggs, grubs, insects, lizards, snakes, fish, yabbies, opossums and larger game – kangaroos, wallabies and emus – all included, but also depended on traditional laws of season and permissions of access. Peramangk people wore very little clothing, especially in summer, but the women were more likely to wear a cloak of opossum fur or kangaroo skin.

Place names within the landscape mark a clear boundary of

Peramangk Territories and their many Clans, even though they also shared many trade items and dreaming across common ground, water, sky and the stars. Art sites along the eastern escarpment and the boundaries defined in the Tjilbruke and Ngarrindjeri song-lines are also part of the Kaurna dreaming.

The ancient beings that carved out this land and the dreaming stories of these beings are still a living presence and known by many of our Meruwatta (Countrymen), Nepo-anna (neighbours) and adjoining Nations, our umbilical cord to cultural ways and country. This will never change, even when the surface of the Earth we all stand on does. Access to Country by foot is part of who we are. We are bound to the land by our heritage, birth rites, dreaming and creator stories; we are the same through our Totems and as the land changes and dies, we die with it.

**Note**

Copley, I. 2015 Story of the Peramangk People. Available at: https://www.ukaria.com/uploads/editor/Story%20of%20the%20Peramangk%20People073802.pdf. Accessed 29 October, 2020.

# Black Thursday

First published anonymously in *Household Words*, edited by Charles Dickens, 10 May 1856, pp. 388–395.

As the voyager approaches the shores of Victoria, the first welcome land which greets him is the bold promontory of Cape Otway. If it be at night, the blaze from the lighthouse on its southern point sends him its cheering welcome for many a league across the ocean which he has so long traversed in expectation, and calls forth rapturous hurrahs from the throng of passengers who crowd to the forecastle. If it be day, the eye rests on its lofty forest hills with a quiet and singular delight. These heights fully respond to the ideal of a new land only recently peopled. Clothed with forests from the margin of the sea to their very summits, they realise vividly the approach to a vast region of primaeval nature. The tall white stems of the gum-trees stand thickly side by side like so many hoary columns; and, here and there amongst them descend dark ravines; while piles of rocks on the heights, alternating with jagged chines and projecting spurs of the mountains, present their solidarity masses to the breeze of ocean.

Amongst the rocks of this wild shore there are sea-caves of vast extent and solemn aspect, which have never yet been thoroughly explored. The forest extending fifty miles or more, in all directions, is one of the most dense and savage in the whole colony. Until lately it was almost impassable from the density of the scrub, and from the thick masses of vines (that is lianas, or creeping cord-like plants, chiefly parasitical), which, as in the forests of South America, climb from tree to tree, knitting the woods into an obscure and impenetrable shade. Excepting along the track from Mr Roadknight's station, near the sources of the Barwon, through the heart of the forest to Apollo Bay, a distance of forty miles, you might cut your way with an axe; but would find it difficult to make progress otherwise. The greater part of the promontory – consisting of steep hills covered with gigantic trees intersected by shelving valleys, and dark with congregated fern-trees, beetling precipices, and stony declivities – affords no food for cattle. In one day, however, known to the colonists as Black Thursday, a hurricane of flame opened its rude and impractical wildernesses to the foot of man: but presented him, at the same time, with a black and blasted chaos of charred trees, and gigantic fallen trunks and branches.

It was in this forest, in the early morning of this memorable day, the sixth of February, eighteen hundred and fifty-one, that a young man opened his eyes and sate up to look about him. He had, the day before, driven a herd of fifty bullocks from the station of Mr Roadknight thus far on his way towards his own residence in the country, between Lake Corangamite and Mount Gellibrand. He had reached at evening a small grassy valley in the outskirts of the forest watered by a creek falling into the western Barwon; and had there paused for the night. His mob of cattle, tired and hungry, were not inclined to stray from the rich pasturage before them; and, hobbling out his splendid black horse Sorcerer, he prepared to pass the night in the simple fashion of the settler on such journeys. A fallen log supplied him with a convenient seat, a fire was quickly lit from the dead boughs which lay plentifully around, and his quart-pot, replenished at the creek was soon hissing and bubbling with its side thrust into the glowing fire. He had a good store of kangaroo-sandwiches and there he sat with his cup of strong bush-tea; looking alternately at the grazing cattle and into the solemn, gloomy, and soundless woods, in which even the laughing-jackass failed to shout his clamorous adieu to the falling day. Only the distant monotone of the morepork – the nocturnal cuckoo of the Australian wilds – reached his ear; making the profound solitude still more solitary. He very soon rolled himself in his travelling-rug, and flung himself down before the fire – having previously piled a fresh supply of timber upon it – near where his trusty dogs lay, and where Sorcerer, in the favourite fashion of the bush-horse, slept as he stood.

The morning was hushed and breathless. Instead of that bracing chill, with which the Australian lodger out of doors generally wakes up, Robert Patterson found the perspiration standing thick on his face, and he felt a strange longing for a deep breath of fresh air. But motion there was none, except in the little creek which trickled with a fresh and inviting aspect at a few yards from him. He arose, and stripping, plunged into the deepest spot of it that he could find; and thus refreshed, rekindled his fire, and made his solitary breakfast. But all around him hung, as it were, a leaden and death-like heaviness. Not a bough nor a blade of grass was moved by the air. The trees stood inanimately moody and sullen. He cast his eyes through the gloomy shadow beneath them, and a sultry, suffocating density seemed to charge the atmosphere. The sky above him was dimmed by a grey haze.

'There is something in the wind to-day, old fellow,' he said, addressing his horse in his usual way; for he had long looked on him as a companion, and firmly believed that he understood all that he said to him. 'There is something in the wind: yet, where is the wind?'

The perspiration streamed from him with the mere exertion of saddling his horse, and, as he mounted him to rouse up his cattle. Horse, dogs, and cattle manifested a listlessness that only an extraordinary condition of the atmosphere could produce. If you had seen the tall, handsome young man seated on his tall and noble horse, you would have felt that they were together formed for any exploit of strength and speed. But the whole troop – cattle, man, and horse – went slowly and soberly along, as if they were oppressed by a great fatigue or the extreme exhaustion of famine.

The forest closed in upon them again, and they proceeded along a narrow track, flanked on each side by tall and densely-growing trees; the creeping vines making of the whole forest one intricate, impenetrable scene. All was hushed as at midnight. No bird enlivened the solitude by its cries, and they had left the little stream. Suddenly there came a puff of air; but it was like the air from the jaws of a furnace, hot, dry, withering in its very touch. The young settler looked quickly in the direction from which it came, and instantly shouted to the cattle before him, in a wild, abrupt, startling shout, swung aloft the stock-whip which he held in his hand, and brought it down with the report of a pistol, and the sharp cut as with a knife, on the ear of a huge bullock just before him. The stock-whip, with a handle about a half a yard long and a thong of three yards long, of plaited bullock-hide, is a terrible instrument in the hands of a practised stockman. Its sound is the note of terror to the cattle, it is like the report of a blunderbuss, and the stockman at full gallop will hit any given spot on the beast that he is within reach of, and cut the piece clean away through the thickest hide that bull or bison ever wore.

He will strike a fly on a spot of mud at full speed, and take away the skin with him, making the rosy blood spring into the wind, and the astonished animal dart forward as if mad.

Loud and louder, wilder and more fiercely shouted the squatter, and dashed his horse forward over fallen trees; through crashing thickets, first on one side of the road, and then on the other. Crack, crack, went the stinging, slashing whip; loud was the bark of dogs; and the mob of cattle rushed forwards at headlong speed. The young man gazed upward; and, through the only narrow opening of the forest, saw strange volumes of smoke rolling southward. Hotter, hotter, stronger and more steadily came the wind. He suddenly checked his horse, and listening, grew pale at the sound which reached him. It was a low deep roar, as of a wind in the tree-tops, or of a heavy water-fall, distant and smothered in some deep ravine.

'God have mercy!' he exclaimed, 'a bush-fire! And in this thick forest!'. Once more he sprang forward, shouting, thundering with his whip. He and the herd were galloping along the narrow wood track. But, as he had turned westward in the direction of his home, the woods – of which he had before seen the boundary – now closed for some miles upon him; and, as he could not turn right or left for the chaos of vines and scrub that the forest, the idea of being overtaken there by the bush-fire was horrible. Such an event would be death, and death only.

Therefore, he urged on his flying herd with desperation. Crack upon crack from his long whip, resounded through the hollow wood. The cattle themselves seemed to hear the ominous sound, and sniff the now strongly perceptible smell of burning. The roar of the fire came louder, and ever and anon seemed to swell and surge, as if urged on by a rough rising blast. The heat was fierce and suffocating. The young squatter's clothes clung to him with streaming perspiration. The horse and cattle steamed and smoked with boiling heat. Yet onward, onward they dashed with lolling tongues. Sorcerer, specked with patches of foam on his dark shining body, seemed to grow furiously impatient of the obstruction offered by the bullocks in his path. As his master's whip exploded on their flanks, he laid back his ears; and, with flaming eyeballs and bared teeth, strove to tear them in his rage.

Robert Patterson knew that the extraordinary heat and drought of the summer had scorched up the grass; the very ground; had licked up the water from crab-hole, pool, and many a creek; had withered the herbage into crisp hay, and so withered the foliage, that you might crumble it between your fingers. The country seemed thoroughly prepared for a conflagration, and only required this fiery wind to send a blaze of extermination over the whole land. For weeks, nay months, the shepherds and sawyers had spoken of fires burning in the hills; and, in the fern-tree breaks of this very forest, he had been recently told that flames had been observed in various directions burning redly by night.

If the fire reached him and his herd before they escaped into the open plains, they must be consumed like stubble. The cattle began to show signs of exhaustion, hanging out their parched tongues, and panting heavily; the perspiration on himself and horse was dried up by the awful heat, and the dogs ran silently, or only whining lowly to themselves, as they hunted every hollow on their way for water. Suddenly, they were out in an open plain, yet with the forest on either hand, but at a considerable distance.

What a scene! The woods were flaming and crackling in one illimitable conflagration. The wind, dashing from the north in gusts of inconceivable heat, seemed to sear the very face and shrivel up the lungs. The fire leaped from tree to tree, flashing and roaring along, with the speed and the destructiveness of

Figure 2. Black Thursday, February 6, 1851. Painting by William Strutt, 1864, courtesy of the State Library of Victoria

lightning. The sere foliage seemed to snatch the fire, and to perish in it in a riot of demoniacal revelry. On it flew, fast as the fleetest horse could gallop; and consuming acres of leaves in a moment, still remained to rage and roar amongst the branches and in the hollow stems of ancient trees. The whole wood on the left was an enormous region of intensest flame; and that on the right, sent forth the sounds of the same ravaging fires; but being to windward, the flames could not be seen for the vast clouds of smoke, mingled with fiery sparks, which were rolled on the air. There was a sound as of thunder, mingled with the crash of falling trees, and the wild cries of legions of birds of all kinds; which fell scorched and blackened and dead to the ground.

Once out on this open plain, the cattle were speedily lost in the blinding ocean of smoke, and the young settler, obliged to abandon them, made a dash onward for his life. Now the flames came racing along the grass with the speed of the wind, and mowing all smooth as a pavement; now it tore furiously through some near point of the forest, and flung burning ashes and tangles of blazing bark upon the galloping rider. But Sorcerer, with an instinct more infallible than human sagacity, sped on, over thicket, and stone, and fallen tree, snorting in the thick masses of smoke and stretching forward his gaping jaws as to catch every breath of air to sustain impeded respiration.

When the wind veered, the reek driven backward, revealed a most amazing scene. The blazing skirts of the forests; huge isolated trees, glaring red – standing columns of fire; here a vast troop of wild horses with flying manes and tails, rushing with thundering hoofs over the plain; there herds of cattle running with bloodshot eyes and hanging tongues, they knew not whither, from the fires; troops of kangaroos leaping frantically across the rider's path, their hair singed and giving out strongly the stench of fire; birds of all kinds and colours shrieking piteously as they drove wildly by, and yet seeing no spot of safety; thousands of sheep standing huddled in terror on the scorched flats, with singed wool, deserted by their shepherds, who had fled for their lives.

But onward flew the intrepid Sorcerer, onward stretched his rider, thinking lightning-winged thoughts of home, and of his helpless, paralysed mother there.

With a caution inspired by former outbreaks of bush-fires, he had made at some distance round his homestead a bare circle. He had felled the trees, leaving only one here and there, at such distances that there was little fear of ignition. As the summer dried the grass, he had set fire to it on days when the wind was gentle enough to leave the flame at command; watching, branch in hand, to beat out any blaze that might have travelled into the forest. By this means, he had hitherto prevented the fire from reaching his homestead; and he had strongly recommended the same plan to his neighbours, though generally with little effect. Now, the fire was so terrible, and sparks flew so wide on the wind, that he feared they might kindle the grass round his homestead, and that he might find everything and every person there consumed.

But, behold! the gleaming, welcome waters of Lake Colac! Sorcerer rushed headlong towards it; and wading hastily up to his sides in its cooling flood, thrust his head to the eyes into it, and drank as if he could never be satisfied with less than the whole lake. Englishmen, new to the scene, would have trembled for the horse; but the bush steed knows best what he needs, eats and drinks as likes him best, and flourishes on it. Smoking hot, the rider lets him drink his fill, and all goes well. The heat produces perspiration, and the evaporation cools and soothes him. Robert

Patterson did not lose a moment in Sorcerer's example. He flung himself headlong from the saddle, dressed as he was, dived, and splashed, and drank exuberantly. He held again and again his smarting face and singed hands in the delicious water; then threw it over the steed, that now, satiated, stood panting in the flood. He laved and rubbed down the grateful animal with wave after wave, cleaning the dried perspiration from every hair, giving him refreshment at every pore. Then up and away again.

He had not ridden two hundred yards, before he saw, lying on the plain, a horse that had fallen in saddle and bridle, and lay with his legs under him, and head stretched stiffy forward, with glaring eye-balls; but dead. Near him was a man, alive, but sunk in exhaustion. His eyes turned wildly on the young squatter, and his parched lips moved, but without a sound. Robert Patterson comprehended his need; and, running to the lake, brought his pannikin full of water, and put it to his mouth. It was the water of life to him. His voice and some degree of strength came quickly back. He had come from the north, and had ridden a race with the fire, till horse and man had dropped here, the horse never to rise again. But Patterson's need was too urgent for delay. He found the man had no lack of provisions he carried him in his arms to the margin of the lake, mounted, and rode on.

As he galloped forward, it was still fire – fire everywhere. He felt convinced that the conflagration – fanned by the strong wind, and acting upon fires in a hundred quarters – extended over the whole sun-dried colony.

It was still early noon, when, with straining eyes, and a heart which seemed almost to stand still with a terrible anxiety, he came near his own home. He darted over the brow of a hill – there it lay safe! The circle within his cleared boundary was untouched by the fire. There were his paddocks, his cattle, his huts, and home. With

a lightning thought his thanks flew up to heaven, and he was the next moment at his door, in his house, in his mother's arms.

Robert's anxiety had been great for the safety of his mother, her anxiety was tripled for him. Terror occasioned by a former conflagration had paralysed her lower extremities; and now, the idea of her only son, her only remaining relative in the colony, being met by this unexampled fire in the dense defiles of the terrible Otway Forest, kept her in a state of the most fearful tension of mind. Mrs Patterson, though confined to her wheeled chair, was a woman of pre-eminent energy and ability. Left with her boy a mere infant, she had managed all her affairs with a skill and discretion that had produced great prosperity. Though her heart was kind, her word was law; and there was no man on her run who dared in the slightest to disobey her; nor one within the whole country round who did not respect and revere her. She had been a remarkably handsome woman. The whole of the floors of the station being built upon one level, in her wheeled chair she could be at any moment in any part of her house or premises.

The moment the first joy of mother and son was over, what a scene presented itself! The station was like a fair. From the whole country round people had fled from the fire, and had instinctively fled there. There was a feeling that the Patterson precautions, which they themselves had neglected, were the guarantees of safety. Thither shepherds had driven their flocks, stockmen their herds, and whole families, compelled to fly from their burning houses, had hurried thither with the few effects that they could snatch up, and bear with them. Patterson's paddocks were crowded with horses and cattle; the bush round his station was literally hidden beneath his own and his neighbour's flocks. Stockmen, shepherds, substantial squatters, now houseless men, were in throngs. Families, with troops of children, had encamped

on the open ground near his house, beneath temporary tents of sheets and blankets. His house was crammed with fugitives, and was one scene of crowding, confusion, and sorrow. Luckily the Patterson store-room was well stocked with flour, and here could be no want of meat with all those flocks and herds about them. But for the cattle themselves there must soon be a famine; and the moment that the fire abated, scouts must be sent off in all directions – but especially to the high plains around Lake Corangamite – in search of temporary pasture. Meantime fires were lighted in a dozen places; and frying-pans and kettles fully employed; for, spite of flight, and loss, and grief, hunger, as Homer thousands of years ago asserted, is impudent, and will be fed.

The stories that the people had to tell were most melancholy. Houses burnt down, flocks destroyed, children suffocated in the smoke or lost in the rapid flight; shepherds and bullock-drivers consumed with their cattle. Numbers had fled to creeks and pools, and yet had been severely burnt; the flames driving over the surface of the water with devouring force. Some had lain in shallow brooks, turning over and over, till finally forced to get up and fly. Still, as the day went on, numbers came pouring in with tales of horror and devastation. The whole country appeared to be the prey of the flames; and men who were, a few hours before, out of the reach of poverty or calamity, were now homeless paupers.

'The Maxwells, mother,' Patterson asked – 'is there any news of them?'

'None, my dear Robert, none,' replied his mother. 'I hope and believe that they are quite safe. They have long ago adopted your own plan of a clearance ring, and I doubt not are just now as much a centre of refuge as we are.'

'But I should like to be sure,' said Robert, seriously. 'I must ride over and see.'

'Must you? I think you need not,' said Mrs Patterson. 'But if you cannot be satisfied, let some one of the men go; there are plenty at hand, and you are already worn out with fatigue and excitement.'

'No, I am quite well and fresh – I had rather go myself,' said Robert; 'it is not far.' And he strode out, his mother saying – 'If you find all right, don't come back to-night.'

Robert Patterson was soon mounted on a fresh and powerful horse, and cantered off towards Mount Hesse. It was only seven miles off. The hot north wind had ceased to blow; the air was cooler, and the fires in the forest were burning more tamely. Yet he had to ride over a track which showed him the ravages which the flames had made in his pleasant woods. The whole of the grass was annihilated; the dead timber lying on the ground was still burning; and huge hollow trees stood like great chimneys, with flames issuing from their tops as from a furnace, and a red intense fire burning within their trunks below; and from them burning earthy matter came tumbling out smoking and rolling on the ground. He was about crossing a small creek, when he saw an Irishman – a shepherd of the Maxwells – sitting on its banks; his clothes were nearly all consumed from his back, his hat was the merest remaining fragment, scorched and shrivelled. The man was rocking himself to and fro and groaning.

'Fehan!' exclaimed Patterson. 'What has happened to you?'

The man turned upon him a visage that startled him with terror. It was, indeed, no longer a human visage; but a scorched and swollen mass of deformity. The beard and hair were burnt away. Eyes were not visible; the whole face being a confused heap of red flesh and hanging blisters. The poor fellow raised a pair of hands that displayed equally the dreadful work of the fire.

The young squatter exclaimed 'How dreadful! Let me help you, Fehan – let me take you home.'

The man groaned again; and, opening his distorted mouth with difficulty and with agony, said:

'I have no home – it is burnt.'

'And your family?'

'Dead – all dead.'

'But are you sure – are you quite sure?' said Robert, excitedly.

'I saw one – my eldest boy: he was lying burnt near the house. I lifted him, to carry him away; but he said, 'Lay me down, father – lay me down; I cannot bear it.' I laid him down, and asked. 'Where are the rest?' 'All fled into the bush,' he said; and then he died. They are all burnt.'

Robert Patterson flung the wretched man a linen handkerchief, bidding him dip it in the creek and lay it on his face to keep the air from it, and turned his horse, saying he would look for the family. He soon found the place where the hut had stood. It was burnt to ashes. On the ground, not far from it, lay the body of the dead little boy. Patterson hastened along the track of the old road to the Maxwells' station, tracing it as well as he could in the fire and the fallen flaming branches. He felt sure the flying family would take that way. In a few minutes it brought him again upon the creek by which the poor man sate, but lower down.

There stood a hut in a damp swamp, which had been used years ago for the sheep washing, but had long been deserted. It was surrounded by thick wattles, still burning. The hut was on fire; but its rotten timbers forcing out far more smoke than flame. As he approached, he heard low cries and lamentations. 'The family is fled thither,' he said to himself, 'and are perishing of suffocation.' He sprang to the ground, and dashed forward through columns of heavy smoke. It was hopeless to breathe in it, for its pungent and stinging strength seemed to close his lungs, and water rushed from his eyes in torrents.

But, pushing in, he seized the first living thing that he laid his hands on, and bore it away. It was a child. Again and again he made the desperate essay, and succeeded in bringing out no less than four children and the mother, who was sunk on the floor as dead, but who soon gave signs of life as she came into the air.

The young man was now in the utmost perplexity with his charge. It was a heart-rending sight. The whole group were more or less burnt; but, as it seemed to him, not so much burnt as to affect their lives. Their station was three miles distant, and he had no alternative but to leave them here till he rode on and sent a cart for them. With much labour, carrying the children one after another in his arms, he conveyed the woeful group to the father.

As the young man stood bewildered by the cries and lamentations of the family on meeting the father, a horse ridden by a lady approached at a gallop. This apparition contrasted strangely with the lamentable group of sufferers. The young lady was tall and of a most beautiful figure, and was mounted on a fine bay horse. A light skirt, and broad felt hat were all the deviations from her home costume that haste had led her to assume. Her face, fresh and roseate, full of youth, loveliness, and feeling, was at the same time grave and anxious, as she gazed in speechless wonder on the scene.

'Miss Maxwell!' Patterson exclaimed, 'in the name of Heaven, what news? How is all at the Mount? Yet, on this dreadful day, what but ill can happen?'

'Nothing is amiss, that I know of,' said the young lady, 'we are safe at home. The fire has not come near us.'

'Thank God!' said Robert. 'I was going to your house, when I fell in with this unfortunate family. Will you ride back and send us a cart?'

'But I beg you will come with me, for I, too, was going to you.'

'To me!' cried the young man, in the utmost astonishment. 'Then all is not right. Is George well?'

'I hope so,' replied Miss Maxwell; but the tears started into her eyes at the same moment, and Robert Patterson gave a groan of apprehension.

'I hope so,' added the young lady, recovering her self-possession; 'but that is the point I want to ascertain. Yesterday, he went with Turcen into the hills to bring in cattle, and this morning the fire surprised them when they had taken two different sweeps along the side of a range. Turcen could not find George again, but made his way home; hoping his master had done the same. George has not yet come, and the fire is raging so fiercely in the hills, that I could think of nothing but coming to you for your advice and assistance.'

'Thank you, Ellen!' said Robert, with a sad emotion. 'I will find him if he be alive.' He sprang upon his horse; and, telling the unhappy family that he would send them immediate assistance, both he and Miss Maxwell galloped away.

We will not attempt to divulge their conversation on the way; but will let you a little into the mutual relations of these two families and these young people. Miss Ellen Maxwell and her brother George were the sole remaining members of their family. As the nearest neighbours of the Pattersons, they had grown into intimate friends. George and Robert had been play-fellows in Van Diemen's Land; and here, where they had come in their boyhood, they were school-fellows. Since then they had gradually grown, from a similarity of tastes and modes of life, the most intimate friends. It was not likely that Robert Patterson and Ellen Maxwell could avoid liking one another. They possessed everything in mind, person, and estate, which made such an attachment the most natural thing in the world. Ellen was extremely attached to Mrs Patterson, for whom she had the highest veneration; Ellen had received an excellent education in Edinburgh, whither she had been sent to her friends. In her nature she was frank, joyous, and affectionate; but not without a keen sense of womanly pride, which gave a certain dignity to her manner, and a reputation for high spirit.

All had gone well between herself and Robert till some six months ago. But, since then, there had sprung up a misunderstanding. Nobody could tell how it had arisen; nobody except Ellen knew; and whatever was the secret cause, she locked it impenetrably within her own bosom. All at once she had assumed a distant and haughty manner towards Robert Patterson. From him she did not conceal that she felt she had cause for dissatisfaction, but she refused to explain. When, confounded at the circumstance, he sought for an explanation, she bade him search his own memory and his heart, and they would instruct him. She insisted that they should cease to regard themselves as affianced, and only consented that nothing as yet should be said on the subject to her brother or Mrs Patterson, on the ground that it would most painfully afflict them.

Ellen, who used to be continually riding over to see Mrs Patterson with her brother, now rarely appeared, and proudly declined to give her reasons for the change in her; adding that she must absent herself altogether, if the subject were renewed. To her brother she was equally reserved; and he attributed her conduct to caprice, bidding Robert take no notice of it. Ellen was not without other admirers; but that was nothing new. One young man, who had lately come into the neighbourhood, paid her assiduous attention, and gossip did not fail to attribute the cause of Robert Patterson's decline of favour to his influence. But Ellen gave no countenance to such a supposition. She was evidently under no desire to pique her old lover by any marked predilection for a new one. Her nature was too noble for the pettiness of coquetry, and any desire to add poignancy to coldness. On the other hand, it was clear to the quietly watchful eye of her brother, that she was herself even more unhappy than Robert. Her eyes often betrayed the effects of secret weeping, and the paleness of her cheek belied the assumed air of cheerfulness that she wore.

Things were in this uncomfortable state at the outbreak of the fire. It was, therefore, a most cheering thought to Patterson that, in her distress, she had flown first, and at once, to him. This demonstrated confidence in his friendship. True, on all occasions, she had protested that her sense of his high moral character was not an iota abated; but, in this spontaneous act, Robert's heart persuaded himself that there lay something more.

No sooner did he reach the Mount, than, leaving Ellen to send off assistance to the Fehans, he took Turcen the stockman, and rode into the forest hills. It was soon dark, and they had to halt; but not far from the spot where Turcen had lost sight of his master. They tethered their horses in a space clear of trees and of fire, and gave them corn that they had brought with them. When the moon rose, they went on to some distance, uttering loud cooees to attract the ear of the lost man; but all in vain. The fire had left the ground hot and covered with ashes, and here and there huge trees burning like columns of red-hot iron.

Finding all their efforts for the night fruitless, they flung themselves down beside their horses; and, with the earliest peep of dawn they were up and off higher into the hills. Their way presented at every step the most shocking effects of the fire.

Ever and anon they came upon bullocks which had perished in it. Here and there, too, they descried the remains of kangaroos, opossums, and hundreds of birds, seared and shrivelled into sable masses of cinder.

They came at length to the spot where Turcen and George Maxwell had parted; and the experienced bushman carefully sought out the tracks of his horses' feet, and followed them. These were either obliterated by the fire, or failed from the rocky hardness of the ground; but, by indefatigable search, they regained them, and were led at length to the edge of a deep and precipitous ravine. In the ravine itself the trees and grass remained unscathed; the torrent of fire had leapt over it, sweeping away, however, every shrub and blade of herb from the heights.

'God defend us!' exclaimed Robert, 'the smoke must have blinded him, and concealed this frightful place. Man and horse are doubtless dashed to pieces.'

He raised a loud and clear cooee; instantly answered by the wild and clamorous barking of a dog; which, in the next instant, was seen leaping and springing about in the bottom of the dell, as if frantic with delight.

'That is Snirrup!' exclaimed Turcen; and the two men began to descend the steep side of the ravine. Robert Patterson outstripped his older and heavier companion. He seemed to fly down the sheer and craggy descent. Here he seized a bough, there a point of the rock, and, in the next instant, was as rapidly traversing the bottom of the glen. Snirrup, the cattle-dog, rushed barking and whining upon him, as in a fit of ecstatic madness, and then bounded on before him. Robert followed in breathless anxiety; stopped the next moment by the sight of George Maxwell's horse, lying crushed and dead. Robert cast a rapid glance around, expecting every moment to see his friend stretched equally lifeless. But presently he heard the faint sound of a human voice.

There lay George stretched in the midst of a grassy thicket, with a face expressing agony and exhaustion. Robert seized his offered hand, and George called first for water. His friend started up and ran down the valley at full speed. He was soon back with a pannikin of water, which the sufferer drank with avidity.

He now learned that, as had been supposed, in the thick smoke, the horse had gone over the precipice, and was killed in an instant. George had escaped, his fall being broken by his steed; and he was flung into the thicket, which again softened the shock of his descent. But he had a broken leg, and was, besides, extremely bruised and torn. Life, however, was strong within him; and Turcen and Robert lost no time in having a litter of poles bound together with stringy bark, made soft with grass and leaves laid in a sheet of the same bark. They had three miles to bear the shattered patient; to whom every motion produced excruciating agonies. It was not long before they heard people in different parts of the wood cooeeing loudly and their answers soon brought not only a number of men, who had been sent out in quest of them, but also Miss Maxwell, herself.

We shall not attempt to describe the sad and yet rejoicing interview of the brother and sister, nor the rapidity with which the different men were sent off upon the horses tied in the hills for the surgeon; who lived two miles off.

In a few days George Maxwell – his leg having been set and his wounds dressed – had become easy enough to relate all that had happened to him; the dreadful night which he had passed in extreme agony in the glen, and the excitement which the loud ringing cooees of Robert, which had reached him, but to which he was unable to reply, had occasioned both him and the faithful and sympathising dog, who barked vehemently, but, as it proved, in vain.

From the moment of this tragic occurrence Robert Patterson was constantly in attendance at the Mount on his friend. He slept in the same room with him, and attended with Ellen as his nurse in the day-time. From this moment the cloud which so long hung over the spirit of Ellen Maxwell had vanished. She was herself again; always kind and open, yet with a mournful tone in her bearing towards Robert, which surprised and yet pleased him. It looked like regret for past unkindness. As they sate one evening over their tea, while George was in a profound sleep in the next room, Ellen, looking with emotion at him, said, in a low, tremulous voice, 'Robert, I owe much to you.'

'To me?' said Robert, hastily. 'Isn't George as much a brother to me as to you?'

'It is not that which I mean,' added Ellen, colouring deeply, yet speaking more firmly; 'it is that I have done you great wrong. I believed that you had said a most ungenerous thing, and I acted upon my belief with too much pride and resentment. I was told that you had jested at me as the daughter of a convict.'

Robert sprang up. 'It is false! I never said it,' he exclaimed. 'Who could tell you such a malicious falsehood?'

'Calm yourself,' added Ellen, taking the young man's hand. 'I shall tell you all.'

'Hear me patiently; for I must impress first on you the strange likelihood of what was reported to me. You were driven to a stockman's hut, it was said, by a storm – you and a young friend. You were very merry, and this friend congratulated you in a sportive style on having won what he was pleased to call the richest young woman in the colony. And with a merry laugh you were made to add, 'and the daughter of the most illustrious of lags!'

Robert Patterson, with a calmness of concentrated wrath, asked, in a low measured tone, 'Who said that?'

'The woman whom you lately saved with all her family. It was Nelly Fehan.'

'Nelly Fehan!' said Robert, in amazement; 'what have I ever done to her that deserved such a stab?'

'You threatened to send Fehan to prison for bush-ranging. You reminded him of his former life and unexpired sentence.'

'That is true,' said Robert, after a pause of astonishment. 'And this was the deadly revenge – the serpents! But, O Ellen! why could you not speak? One word, and all would have been explained.'

'I could not speak, Robert. Wounded pride silenced me. But I have suffered severely; have been fearfully punished. I can only say – forgive me!'

One long embrace obliterated the past.

The late Mr Maxwell had been transported for the expression of his liberal political principles in hard and bigoted times. There was not a man in the penal settlement, who did not honour his political integrity and foresight, and who did not reverence his character. But the convicts as a body were proud to claim him as of their own class, though sent thither only for the crime of a Hampden or a Sidney. Whenever reproach was thrown on the convict section of society, the insulted party pointed to the venerable exile, and triumphantly hailed him as their chief. No endeavours, though they were many, and conducted by powerful hands, had ever been able to procure a reversal of his sentence. The injuries of a man of his high talents and noble nature might be comparatively buried at the antipodes; at home they would be a present, a perpetual and a damaging reproach. He had lived and died a banished, but a highly-honoured man. Still, as he rose to a higher estimation and an unusual affluence, there were little minds who delighted occasionally to whisper – 'After all, he is but a lag.' And it was on this tender point that the minds of his children, whose ears such remarks had reached and wounded, had become morbidly sensitive.

Amid the general calamity, this reconciliation was like a song of thanksgiving in the generous heart of Robert Patterson, and quickened it to tenfold exertions in alleviating the sufferings of his neighbours. His joy was made boundless and overflowing by a circumstance which appeared to be little short of a miracle. When Robert rode up to his own station, he beheld his mother – not seated in her wheeled chair – but on foot; light, active, and alert, going to and fro amongst the people whose destitution still kept them near his house. The mass of misery that she saw around her and the exertion which it stimulated burst the paralytic bonds which had enchained her for years. The same cause which had disabled her limbs had restored them.

The conflagration had extended over a space of three hundred miles by a hundred and fifty, and far away beyond the Goulburn, the Broken River, and the Ovens, we have witnessed the remaining traces of its desolation. Over all this space, flocks and herds in thousands had perished. Houses, ricks, fences and bridges had been annihilated. Whole families had been destroyed. Solitary travellers, flying through the boundless woods before the surging flame, had fallen and perished. For weeks and months, till the kindly rains of autumn had renewed the grass, people journeying through the bush beheld lean and famishing cattle, unable to rise from the ground, and which by faint bellowings seemed to claim the pity and aid of man. Perhaps no such vast devastation ever fell on any nation; and the memory of Black Thursday is an indelible retrospect in Victoria.

# Better Prospects are Ahead

The short story 'Black Thursday', published on May 10, 1856 in Charles Dickens' weekly journal *Household Words,* brought the terror of Australian bushfires to an English reading public. While published anonymously, it is the story of a young pastoralist driving a herd of 50 bullocks through one of the first recorded bushfires in Australia, when approximately 5 million hectares of the colony of Victoria burnt on 6 February 1851. It was written by William Howitt[1] from stories told to him after he arrived in Australia in 1852, although students of Dickens will nonetheless recognise a Dickensian style of writing and turn of phrase. Though published 165 years ago, its evocation of the 1851 bushfire poignantly establishes the setting for the stories told in this book.

The village of Prospect Hill is located near the country township of Meadows in the District Council of Mount Barker, southeast of Adelaide in South Australia. Today, it is a cluster of museums and community service buildings. Only known by this name since 1873, Prospect Hill was a farming-oriented community, with a life centred around dairying, sawmilling and various forms of agriculture. Backing on to the Kuitpo forest, a

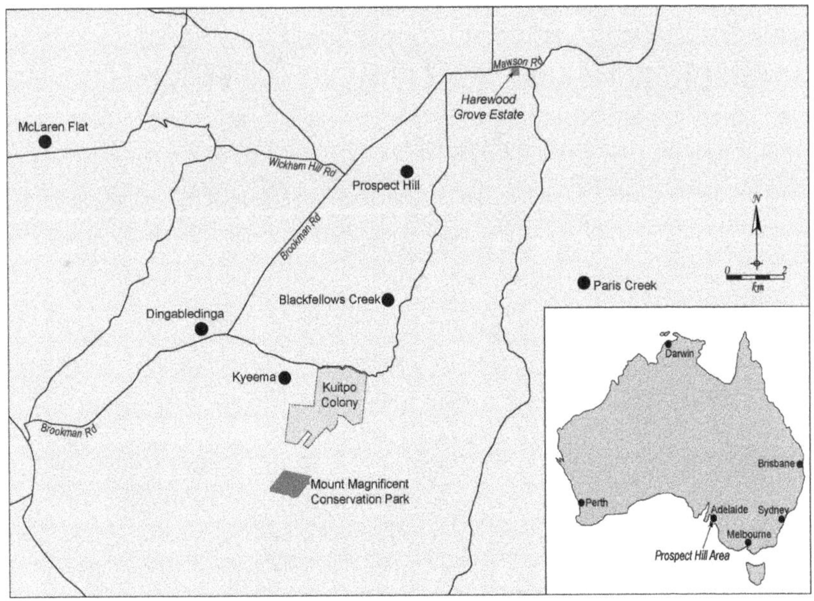


Figure 3. Location of Prospect Hill. Map drawn by Fiona Brady.

large pine plantation established in 1899, Prospect Hill is also highly susceptible to bushfires. The stories that lie at the heart of this book recall a major fire event that seared through the lives of the people in this small South Australian town over three decades ago: the now infamous 'Ash Wednesday' bushfires that erupted in the 16th February 1983. So severe were these fires across South Australia and Victoria that 'Ash Wednesday' became a byword for natural disaster and is counted as the most devastating bushfire event of the late 20th century. These are more than just memories of things past. Prospect Hill's experiences of Ash Wednesday, and of how they chose to deal with its aftermath as individuals and as a community, speak to three closely interwoven and significant contemporary issues. The first is the ways in which the past in

Figure 4a. Prospect Hill township, 13 October, 2020. Photo: Jiayuan Liang.

Figure 4b. Aerial photograph of Prospect Hill, 15 November, 2020.
Photo: Jiayuan Liang.

all its myriad forms, including historic buildings and objects and the memories of places and events, create for a community a core sense of identity that is both stable and ever changing. The second is how cultural heritage – the material and immaterial traces of that past, especially the stories that are told about it – can be used to build, foster and enhance community resilience. The final and perhaps most critical issue, and one that speaks directly to the memories and stories of bushfires, is the risk of human-induced climate change, that is shifting the weather into more unpredictable and ever more extreme patterns.

## Life Histories of a Community

Each town has its own stories. Prospect Hill is in many ways a typical small rural community. An application for the first survey of the area was submitted on 31st January, 1839, only two years and one month after South Australia was initially colonised by the British. The first survey was by Deputy Surveyor-General Thomas Burr in the 1840s. During the middle of the nineteenth century it became a farming district, settled by English, Scottish and Irish colonists. During this period, the principal industries were dairying, agriculture and sawmilling. Early crops included wheat and tobacco and early occupations included shingle cutting, roof thatching, pit sawing, blacksmithing, charcoal burning and wattle barking. Today, the principal industry is dairying.

Like the world at large, Prospect Hill is in a constant state of becoming. The stories in this book provide insights into a world that was more stable, more predictable and seemingly more enduring than that which we inhabit today. In 1871 the population of the area was 154 people. By 1938 this had increased to around 450. Today it has a population of 159. A key thread is how to build and nurture a community despite population fluctuations, particularly the role of small community organisations in providing a means for people to work towards shared goals. Some institutions have diminished or disappeared through time, while others have endured. Brenda Nisbett recalls the centrality of the church to social and ceremonial life, especially the times when night services were put on for special occasions. The Country Women's Association organised and catered for community events, including Brenda and Graeme Nisbett's wedding. The Scouts Association provided the means for young people to obtain critical skills in bushcraft and survival. While the Country Women's Association at Prospect Hill no longer exists, in 2021 the Scouts Association has had 77 years of uninterrupted scouting in Prospect Hill. Over the years, tennis, table-tennis and photography also provided opportunities for community building. Pat Connor recollects the pleasure of going to a weekly dance and occasionally to church. He recalls people spending time visiting neighbours and talking to each other, discussing what happened during the week. And there are brushes with fame. Sir Douglas Mawson, the scientist and Antarctic explorer, once owned a 1200-acre property, named Harewood, in the area, his presence now memorialised in Mawson Road, Meadows.

This book presents a synthesis of major themes in oral histories concerning the European settlement of Prospect Hill, namely the pioneering days, community spirit, the industries that helped the town take root; some of the places and objects that are important to the residents of Prospect Hill residents and, of course, the personalities who each had a vast impact on the development of the town. Taken together, these themes represent a recipe for a cohesive community. Every successful community would have a handful of these things, but what is significant in Prospect Hill is just how fragile they are in a changing, modernising world. Small villages like Prospect Hill are at risk of being urbanised or abandoned altogether. For example, what would once have been a difficult job clearing scrub is now made easier by better technology; the community spirit, while still present, is lessened by digital media, and a declining, ageing population; and the industries that were once at the core of the community, like dairy farming, have been greatly impacted by new technology and a capitalist system that does not work in the farmer's favour.

The stories in this book allow us to identify major changes in society and to lay the shape of our lives today over the contours of the challenges faced by people in the past. Joyce Smart recalls an uncle whose wife had twins – both of whom died – and who passed away soon afterwards, leaving the father to care for seven children. Without any form of government support to draw on, he collected witchetty grubs and walked almost 80 kilometres (one way) to Wellington to sell them to fisherman so he could buy food. There were advantages, too. While people today are routinely burdened by mortgages – some of which are now intergenerational – Deane Michelmore speaks of people building their own houses 'out of ... the natural materials that were there'. We learn of major changes in industries that include the reduction of around 35-40 dairy farms to only two, and of a 'really big' wattle bark industry that is non-existent today, the purpose of which is almost beyond the reach of memory.

The landscapes around Prospect Hill are inscribed with romance, adventure and tragedy. Deane Michelmore describes a flowering gum known as 'the parting tree', the point at which boys would reluctantly take leave of their girlfriends when escorting them from church or community events. Ray Bailey speaks of a large tree known as Flagtree, which had a flagpole at its crown that alerted settlers to the movements of ships as part of a semaphore (telegraphic communication) system extending from Adelaide to Encounter Bay. One of the most poignant stories is told by Ray Bailey. He recounts the death of Sarah McHarg, who regularly stayed with the wife of the Governor-Surveyor, Henry Burr, when he was away from home surveying:

> Now the distance between the two camps was only about five kilometres, but she was escorted through the scrub. But one day, Sarah, for some reason, decided she wanted to go back to her parents' camp and ... she simply disappeared. Her remains were not found for some two years at Currency Creek, and it was a very sad business because she had built herself a little wurley, she made a bed out of reeds, and she had left a message to her mother and her sister. I cannot recall all the words, but one was more or less her last will and testament where she had asked that her effects be left to, originally to her mother, but then to one of her sisters. And it is said that he had left a message to one of her sisters: 'Grieve not for me, as I am resigned to my fate.' (Ray Bailey, 18 November 2014)

This book is peppered with memorable characters. We are introduced to Miss Adelaide Mary Galley, the teacher who taught 42 students across seven grades in a single classroom, and to a man named Archie, who drowned while trying to cross the flooded creek whilst drunk. His tragic end is memorialised in Archie's Bridge, located on Black Nursery Road. We learn of the trials, hopes and tribulations of different generations of the settler families who stayed in the area for generations: the Griggs family, the Harvey family, the Connors, the Michelmores, the Brookmans, Oakleighs, Lochiers, Stones and Milligans. Jack Lovelock recalls his grandfather's early life after being taken on by Mr Griggs as a helper when only ten years of age following the death of his own father. When his grandfather went on his first trip to the markets at Adelaide, he was asked if he was 'Mr Griggs' man'. When he confirmed this, the man to whom he was talking called to the others, 'Come and have a look at Mr Griggs' man: a ten-year-old boy!'

There are absences, as well, most notably the experiences of Peramangk people. While an Aboriginal presence is still present in landmarks, particularly Blackfellows Creek and the fire station that is now located there, there are only a few glimpses of Aboriginal people. Joyce Smart and Ray Bailey recall stories of Aboriginal people moving through the landscape on a seasonal basis, camping around Blackfellows Creek and moving to the more hospitable plains during winter. Joyce recollects finding cockle shells left by Aboriginal people who had travelled up from the sea, and Graeme Usher remembers 'middens of mussel shells, metres deep where obviously they'd been for a long time'. These are only traces, however, of rich lives lived in the area of Prospect Hill over thousands of years. The absence among European settler families of oral histories about Aboriginal people tells its own story, one in which the Aboriginal population was reduced drastically after contact as a result of starvation, disease and violence, and, after that, of lives that rarely intersected.

**Black Friday, Ash Wednesday**

Prospect Hill has a long history of being confronted by bushfires during the hot and dry summer months of January and February each year. The first life-threatening fire known for this region was in 1859 around Mt Barker and Macclesfield.[2] Other major blazes occurred in 1900 around Mt Barker and in 1901, including the area around Prospect Hill.[3] These were followed by bushfires in

Figure 5. Lindsay Gibson at the ruins of the Dining Hall of Kuitpo Colony Camp 2. 15 November, 2013. Photo: Jiayuan Liang.

Kuitpo Forest in 1931 and in the general region in 1933.[4] Six years later another series of fires tore through the Adelaide Hills in January 1939, burning across large swathes around Macclesfield and Meadows, although without quite reaching Prospect Hill itself. Temperatures in the high 40s, combined with high winter and autumn rainfall and a spring drought, resulted in five days of bushfires. Approximately 575,000 hectares of reserved forest and 780,000 hectares of forested Crown land burnt, along with over 1,000 homes, and 71 people lost their lives.[5] In the vivid and ominous naming tradition for such events this became known as 'Black Friday'. Among other things, it led to the establishment of the Emergency Fire Services as a branch of the Police Department.

Such events are sadly repetitious. In 1980 severe bushfires destroyed 51 homes in the Adelaide Hills and only a few years later, on Wednesday, 16th February 1983, more than 200 square

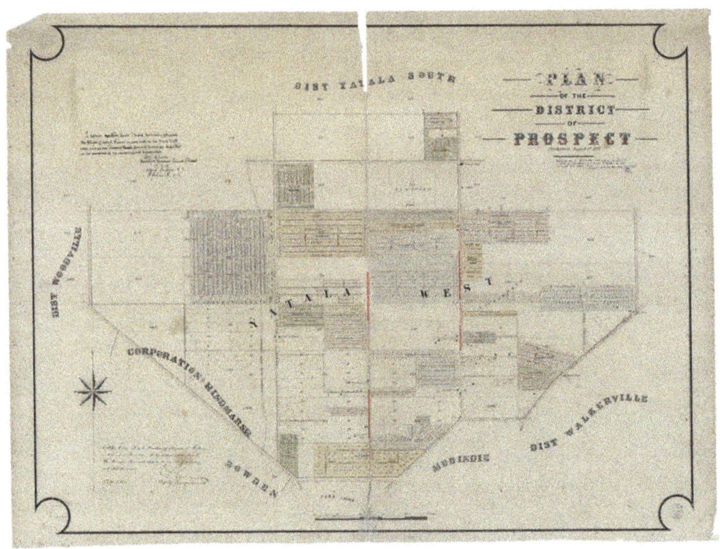


Figure 6. Plan of the district of Prospect [cartographic material]: proclaimed August 1st 1872, 1872-1879, map/chart, courtesy State Library of South Australia.

km of South Australia burned, including the Mt Lofty Ranges on the metropolitan fringe of Adelaide and a large area immediately south and southwest of Meadows and Macclesfield that included Prospect Hill. These were the Ash Wednesday bushfires that killed 75 people across Victoria and South Australia. So severe was this conflagration that 'Ash Wednesday' became a byword for natural disaster, and the most devastating bushfire of the late 20th century.

Two of the people who died were visiting in the area near Prospect Hill. Jane Winifred Gregurke, aged 24, and Warren John McCourt, aged 23, from the Adelaide suburb of Ascot Park, were house sitting the property Orangebank while the owners, Jenny and John Bogarts, were on their honeymoon at Kangaroo

Figure 7. Views of the Ash Wednesday bushfire from Glenys and Graeme Usher's home, 16 February, 1983, courtesy Glenys and Graeme Usher.

Island. It still confounds local people that the young couple died when the house collapsed while the animals in the yards outside survived.

Memories of the 1983 disaster still resonate in the lives of the inhabitants of Prospect Hill, highlighting what they lost and what they saved, and their responses to the disruptions that fire wrought to the landscape, animal life, households and lives. The emotional landscape of 'home' in this sense is broader than just a house, encompassing the places people worked in and walked in, as well as the larger community they knew intimately. Home ties together ideas, feelings, expectations and histories in ways that shape relationships between people and the world. When the emotional landscape of home – at whatever scale – is at risk by natural disaster all of these aspects of life come under threat.

In this book we learn about fire behaviours from people who fought fires that could not be imagined. Graeme Usher observes that 'the fire itself broke all existing fire behaviour knowledge that we knew at the time' and that 'we had never even imagined the intensity of it ... [it] was such an intense fire it made its own conditions'. Caught in its midst, Joyce Smart was able to draw on her intimate knowledge of her own lands to find the one spot in 72 acres where she and her animals might survive.

The contrast between the burnt and the unburnt underscored people's ongoing relationships with the town, and the sense of co-operation and solidarity that emerged from such a shared experience shapes several of the recollections contained in this volume. For Deane Michelmore Ash Wednesday transformed Prospect Hill from a relatively unknown backwater to a community well known for its cohesion and resilience: 'before Ash Wednesday, it was a quiet little town, well known within a certain circle but probably not much out of that but since Ash Wednesday and everything that has happened since, it's become far better known as an example, I guess, of rebuilding a community.'

In these circumstances heritage particularly came to the fore. In editing these stories, we were particularly struck by the way in which the community chose to look backwards in order to move forwards. This was not done apprehensively, but in a way that respected the past and the events that shaped it. In a sense, the community took solace in its history and used its social identity as a rallying point to rebuild their lives. Many allude to the ways in which the shared efforts of a community recovering and rebuilding its heritage contributed to healing. For Deane Michelmore:

> ... the thing that stands out most of all to me in relation to the aftereffects of the bushfire is the way that catastrophe certainly pulled everybody together to a much greater degree. Just after

> Ash Wednesday, Malcolm Slade and a few other people organised basically a wake. I think pretty well everybody in Prospect Hill turned out that night. It was held on the tennis courts (Deane Michelmore, 5 March, 2014).

During the fire the town lost several public buildings and many houses, as well as elements of historical value that could never be replaced: 'We've lost a lot of history. One that I can really see that sticks out ... is when the CWA [Country Women's Association] Hall went up in smoke. We had the Burman lending library in there. Well, that was part of the history of the district – that's been lost. You can't ever replace things like that' (Glenys Usher, 18 November 2014). Ray Bailey and others note the concerted efforts that have been put into protecting and preserving the built heritage of Prospect Hill since then, particularly the love, care and attention that has been devoted to the Museum. Glenys Usher recalls how the bushfire display in the museum helped people to vent feelings that they thought 'buried and gone' and Joyce Smart describes the emotional connection that helped her to find solace in its objects. Although once owned by others, these ordinary artefacts of daily life helped her to repair the breach caused by losing her own house in the blaze:

> Being a hoarder, and a sentimentalist, I had nothing of my stuff left: anything that I'd ever had from when I was a child ... I lost all of those things. I never had anything old or anything that Mum had given me, and to be able to come over here [to the Museum] and ... to live amongst the ... old things ... it helped me – it helped me a lot. It still does. Even if it is a struggle ... it's the most important part of my life. (Joyce Smart, 12 March 2014)

## Aboriginal cultural burning

The final portions of this book were compiled in the aftermath of the bushfires that ravaged the southeastern Australia from December 2019 through to February 2020, and while wildfires were raging in California and other parts of the western United States. It wasn't always this way. Over the 60,000 years that they have lived on the Australian continent Aboriginal people developed cultural practices that enabled them not only to live with fire but also to use it as a tool to manage the environment. In northern Australia, these behaviours were noted by the archaeologist Rhys Jones, in a paper that argued that 'fire-stick farming' by Aboriginal people changed the nature, season and frequency of fires as part of a system of resource management[6]. Jones' work prompted research on the frequency of fires in order to establish the timing of the initial Indigenous occupation of Australia.[7] While Jones' view that Aboriginal people were managing their environments was radical at the time, today it is widely accepted.

While there has been disagreement about the degree to which Aboriginal burning changed or augmented the natural fire regime, no-one has argued that the megabushfires of today are a natural part of Australia's fire regime. The charcoal records show no evidence of widespread catastrophic fires. Whenever there are bushfires in Australia, Aboriginal people, anthropologists and archaeologists call for a return to cultural burning practices and for recognition of the depth and value of Aboriginal traditional ecological knowledge. Aboriginal cultural burning is low-intensity. Fires burn in a mosaic pattern, like a chessboard, which allows even the smallest or least mobile animals to move between areas. Afterwards, the burnt hollows of trees provide homes for selected animal species. Some plants, such as the tree fern (*Dicksonia Antarctica*), have adapted so they regenerate after burning.

Estimates of increased risk from climate induced change predict that bushfires will become both more intense and more frequent over coming decades, forcing a greater awareness of the consequences of current actions and a greater focus on human-nature centred futures. This will require ingenuity, resilience and action on all our parts and a wider acceptance of alternative ways of seeing and understanding the Australian bush.

There are aesthetic considerations as well. The colours of bushfire have long haunted the imagination of non-Indigenous Australia. From the names given to various major conflagrations – Black Thursday (1851), Black Friday (1939), Black Saturday (2009), Ash Wednesday (1983) – to the emotions elicited by seeing a landscape transformed by burning, the colours of fire – red, orange, black and grey – are used regularly to represent devastation. In Aboriginal systems of knowledge, however, these colours are part and parcel of caring for traditional country, and to reduce them to a label for a major disaster is highly offensive. A white-skinned tourist once said that the landscape after a reduction burn, to her, looked black and dirty. She was so repulsed that she planned to make representations to politicians to ban the system. In contrast, to Phyllis Wiynjorroc, the senior Traditional Owner of the Bagula clan lands of the Jawoyn people in the Northern Territory, the post-burn landscape looked 'nice and clean', signalling country that was well cared for and highly valued. We see such colours through a cultural lens and how we interpret colour is often unconscious.

The challenge of climate change over coming decades will be to rethink our assumptions and find new and better ways to engage with the colours of a burnt and burning landscape. While early artists emulated the soft greens of England, Australian-born artists typically depicted the landscape in soft palettes of

Figure 8. Fred Williams. *After bushfire (1)* 1968 gouache 57.0 x 76.6 cm (image and sheet) National Gallery of Victoria, Melbourne. Purchased through The Art Foundation of Victoria with the assistance of the H.J. Heinz II Charitable and Family Trust, Governor, and the Utah Foundation, Fellow, 1980 (AC9-1980) © Estate of Fred Williams.

blue, green and gold, as in Frederick McCubbin's, *The Pioneer* and *On the Wallaby Track*; Hans Heyson's *Mystic Morn* and *Droving in the Light,* Tom Roberts' *I Break Away!* and Arthur Streeton's *Golden Summer.* Fred Williams was one of the few Australian-born artists who grappled with the aesthetics of a bushfire landscape. His celebrated bushfire series was prompted by a blaze that stopped only 100 metres short of his home in February 1968. This experience fundamentally altered Williams' vision of the Australian landscape. His artistic response was a detailed and repeated focus on burnt landscapes that helped to reshape Australian perceptions of bushfire. Like Fred Williams, we will have to alter our appreciation of what an Australian environment looks like. As we explore links between bushfires and climate change we need to monitor when the landscapes around us are being blackened through appropriate forms of burning. Adopting Indigenous wisdom and attitudes about cultural burning could help us to become more aware of when and where regular burning practices are being implemented, as well as its opposite: those areas where regular burning is not taking place. There is more than one kind of blackened landscape. If we can learn to love the right kind, we might be able to limit our experience of the other.

**Last words**

This manuscript was completed the day after the report by the Royal Commission into National Natural Disaster Arrangements[8] was tabled in the Australian Parliament on 30th October, 2020. The commission was established in response to the extreme bushfire season in 2019-2020 which resulted in devastating loss of life, property and wildlife, and environmental destruction across Australia and in relation to the changing global climate. Major recommendations encourage acknowledgement of the role of Indigenous fire managers in mitigating bushfire risks:

> Recommendation 18.1 Indigenous land and fire management and natural disaster resilience Australian, state, territory and local governments should engage further with Traditional Owners to explore the relationship between Indigenous land and fire management and natural disaster resilience.
>
> Recommendation 18.2 Indigenous land and fire management and public land management Australian, state, territory and local governments should explore further opportunities to

leverage Indigenous land and fire management insights, in the development, planning and execution of public land management activities.

In many respects the story of Prospect Hill is a tale repeated across Australia and one that is emblematic of small rural communities, although the narratives of such small settlements are rarely captured in the big picture stories of early Australia. Though it is still a rural community, Prospect Hill is no longer isolated. It changed over the course of the twentieth century, as the distance between it and Adelaide was reduced through the introduction of faster, cheaper and better cars, wider and speedier roads. While some of the people who live there today are descendants of the original settlers, many of the children of Prospect Hill families have chosen to live elsewhere and their places have been taken by newcomers. Jack Lovelock observes that 'we've got a lot of new people ... they wave to me on the road as they go by, but I don't know their names, you know? There's a lot of people I don't know. Whereas, years ago, I knew everybody.' There are concomitant changes in how people interact. Graeme Usher notes, that 'people have become very time poor', and much of their attention has become focused on the city rather than the town.

Although the name Prospect Hill did not come into use until 1873,[9] optimism has underlain the attitudes of the residents of the town for nearly two centuries. The 1870s marked a major shift for the village when a new church was built, a general store opened and – wonder of modern travel – a spring cart service to and from Adelaide commenced. An early resident, Miss Cross, captured the feeling of buoyancy that accompanied these developments with the chance remark that 'Better prospects are ahead'.In considering the future of Prospect Hill we defer to residents Joyce Smart and Keith Griggs:

> Prospect Hill – it's the best place on earth. And I think that you would have heard Keith say, 'If Prospect Hill means as much to you as it means to me, there will always be a Prospect Hill.' (Joyce Smart, 12 March 2014).

Even the everyday histories of ordinary townships can have extraordinary moments.

**Notes**

1 Howitt, W. 1857. *Tallangetta. The Squatter's Home. A Story of Australian Life*. London: Longman, Brown, Green, Longmans, & Roberts. Available at: https://archive.org/details/tallangettasquat01howi/page/n7/mode/2up

2 *South Australian Weekly Chronicle*, 12 February 1859, p. 5.

3 *Mount Barker Courier and Onkaparinga and Gumeracha Advertiser* 2 February 1900, p. 3; *Advertiser* 30 March 1901, p. 8.

4 *Advertiser and Register* 26 February 1931, p. 9; *Advertiser* 23 February 1933, p. 9.

5 Forest Fire Management Victoria 2017.

6 Jones, R. 1969 Firestick farming. *Australian Natural History* 16: 224–231.

7 Gill, A.M., R.H. Groves and I.R. Noble 1981 *Fire and the Australian Biota*. Canberra: Australian Academy of Science.

8 Royal Commission into National Natural Disaster Arrangements 2020 Royal Commission into National Natural Disaster Arrangements Report. Canberra: Commonwealth of Australia. Available at: https://naturaldisaster.royalcommission.gov.au/publications/royal-commission-national-natural-disaster-arrangements-report

9 Harvey, Syd, Pat Conor and Keith Griggs 1973. *Golden Days. From Golden Days to Fields of Green. The Centenary of Prospect Hill*. Adelaide: Commercial Publications of South Australia Ltd for the Prospect Hill Centenary Celebrations, 1973.

# Deane Michelmore

Figure 9. Deane Michelmore, 5 March, 2014. Photo: Antoinette Hennessy.

I lived in the Prospect Hill area for 62 years. We moved away in 1990, came to Victor Harbor. So that means that I have been in Victor Harbor, within a month or so, 24 years.

My house in Prospect Hill was located on a property called *Sunnybrae*. My main occupation was as a dairy farmer. But I did some earth moving work as well, and transport. Earth moving/fodder conservation contractor. We used to do quite a lot of fodder conservation around the district. Many years ago, most of the farms through Prospect Hill and Blackfellows Creek, Kuitpo and nearby areas were dairy farms. Dairy farming was probably the main thing, and potato growing; they were probably the two main agricultural projects that happened around that area. It is interesting that today, to the best of my knowledge, there's only two dairy farms left in that Prospect Hill area; compared with many, many, many years ago. But that's a sign of the times.

The Michelmore family first came down on Meadows South, west of Prospect Hill, in 1840. Our property, Gum View, is located south of Meadows and west of Kuitpo Forest Headquarters. I have been told by my uncle Hedley that when my ancestors first came out from England, when they left Devon, they lived under a big gum tree for a while. It was a big red gum tree. It is still there and I could take you to it. They felled some timber and made a shack to live in. That old fireplace that they built, I can still recall. They used to drag logs to the door with horses. Then, instead of cutting the logs up, they would push the logs in through the door, into the fire. As it burned the ends of the logs off, they would just keep pushing the logs into the fire. So whilst it might have saved cutting the wood, they had to push the logs instead. Unfortunately, that building or that property got burned several years ago. Later they built a house there out of stone, but unfortunately it all got destroyed. It is a heritage site though, which is a good thing.

There is still a small portion of the house still standing (part of the dining room). It was a big dining room because there were nine children. My grandmother, Sarah, had nine children that survived, all boys. Sarah had one daughter who died when she was a toddler. Sarah made sure that each one of those nine surviving children learned a trade. She also purchased properties of 150-200 acres for each of them. She was part-Chinese and she married a Michelmore. That is why her oldest son was called Hedley Looney Ching Michelmore.

My grandfather lived there. He was the one that came out from England. I never knew my grandfather. He passed away a fairly young man. So my grandmother brought up those nine children – two children were deceased – which I think was a fantastic effort.

My parents built a house. First of all, my father built a little shack near a well that he dug. He lived in that shack while he built the house that still exists today. They used ironstone rubble which is nearby, probably within 50 to 100 metres from the house. They used the ironstone rubble to make concrete for the house and then they plastered over the concrete afterwards. In those days and pretty well all through the state people built houses out of the natural materials that were on site, and that's what they did.

We have still got a son living there. My son went on the property that I lived on for a start after I came to Victor Harbor. But that got sold and he moved out of the district. Our property was called Sunnybrae, which is section 3410, Hundred of Kuitpo, towards Blackfellows Creek. The creek is named Norris Creek. Previous to that, the property was owned by the Norris family, two bachelor brothers. It was then owned by my grandmother, then my father – who developed it, or developed most of it – and then myself. We sold that property probably about eight years ago, in 2006.

I can still remember the ruins of the old cottage. There was an old fig tree there, I can recall that. And an old plum tree down towards the creek, I can still recall that. None of that is there now, of course. Purely because I pushed it away. I still remember the heap of rubble which was where the cottage was. That got the stone for the cottage from the other side of the creek. There was a hill that was full of rubble. Later, I finished carting most of it away as rubble for various properties around the district – including the base for the second tennis court built at Prospect Hill, which was built after Ash Wednesday. All that base rubble came out of that quarry.

One of the features of Sunnybrae was some huge, huge red gum trees growing along that creek. When I say huge, two or three of the stumps were still there when I took the property over. I remember measuring one of them and it was eight feet in diameter. That's a big tree. There is still one of those large trees left on the property. I have been told it is one of the tallest red gum trees in the Mt. Lofty Ranges. I don't have any proof of that. I was told that by an employee of the Electricity Trust several years ago. And that tree is big enough. I remember when I was growing up, two horses could get inside the burnt out part of the tree. You wouldn't see the horses. You could see their tail swishing, that's all you'd see. They used to do that on a very hot day. They would go in that tree in the shade. This was a good thing for the horse, wasn't it?

Talking about the big trees, that brings me to those trees that had been cut down. They cut them down and used them to mill for railway sleepers. Of course, in those days they didn't have the modern mills that we've got today. They would dig a pit. There were two pits on Sunnybrae. They would then put a couple of logs across the pit that they'd dug. They would put a couple of bearers on there – in other words, a couple of logs, smaller logs – and then they would roll the big logs onto the bearers. Then they would saw that big log into sleepers using a big cross-cut saw. One man was up on top of the log and one man was down in the pit. That's the way they would cut the sleepers out many, many years ago. I still recall that when I was younger one of those big logs was left on the property, not far from one of the pits. Apparently, the sledge, or however they were carting it down the gully, down on Norris' Creek, got bogged and they couldn't move. So they rolled the log off and left it there. That log was there for many, many, many years. Until, unfortunately, one day my father was burning some gorse bushes nearby and a spark got into that log. It burnt all of the log. Which was a shame. I wish it was still there, just as a record. But that's how it goes. I must admit I filled the pits in later, which I regret now. I should have marked where the pits were, shouldn't I?

In the past, Prospect Hill was – and still is, to the best of my knowledge – a very, very close-knit community. A very close-knit community with a community spirit.

The first thing that I remember is going to Prospect Hill Methodist Church with my parents. I guess it must have been mainly a Methodist community for the community to build a Methodist church. Way back in those days, churches were one of the first public buildings that were built in many, many, many places, throughout the world for that matter. Prospect Hill was mainly Methodist, but not entirely, of course. We used to go to church in a horse and buggy. I still remember the old carbide lights, on the side of the buggy. My grandmother Sarah used to take her nine sons to the Prospect Hill Church. She was a very, very strong, strict woman. There was never any nonsense in the Michie house. My grandmother was the wife of Charles. She and Mrs Alec Connor, who lived next door to the church, gave the

Figure 10. Kuitpo Hall, built 1926. 23 November, 2020. Photo: Jiayuan Liang

money for the Soldiers War Memorial plaque in the Prospect Hill Church grounds.

Our house was approximately a half a mile (in the language of those days) from Blackfellows Creek Road and at the foot of Bee Tree Hill. It was called that because obviously it was a big tree years ago and it had bees in it, so it got named Bee Tree Hill. We go further towards Prospect Hill through or past Wattle Gully, which was the next gully. It was called Wattle Gully because of all the wattles that naturally grew in that area. After Ash Wednesday those seeds were still there because they came up by the millions. My brothers and sisters and I would go to Prospect Hill Sunday School. Then we used to have lunch with somebody at Prospect Hill. Most times it was the Griggs family, the George Griggs family. Then we went back home after that.

I first went to school at Kuitpo. Kuitpo School was in the Kuitpo Hall. Kuitpo Hall was built as a result of the community that was set up in Kuitpo during the planting of Kuitpo Forest. Kuitpo Colony was set up during the Depression by a Methodist Minister, the Reverend Samuel Forsyth. It was set up to give people work during the Depression when they couldn't get work. It catered for many, many people out there. They had work clearing the scrub, cutting a lot of timber, which used to get sold to brick kilns and so on. They used to cut wood and various things like that because, in those days, wood was a sellable item to the brick kilns and places like that. I and a lot of other people carted many, many tons of kiln wood down to Adelaide, to Halletts and to other companies for their brick kilns. We also carted kiln wood over to Littlehampton to the brick kiln there, which incidentally is still there today. Many of the huts, cottages and houses are still there. They set up a pottery because they had a good clay deposit. The pottery worked very well for quite a while and used to supply the Adelaide market, plus others. They also set up their own slaughterhouse, the butcher side of it, to supply their own meat. Also, they set up their own poultry sheds and the slaughterhouse.

Kuitpo Colony was a very, very independent organisation which really served a purpose at that period of time. Later on, it was used as a respite centre for people who were alcoholics. They could go out there and recuperate. It served that purpose for quite a long while. I understand it is still serving that purpose, but on a much, much smaller scale.

Some of the names that I remember that were in the Prospect Hill area were the Pearces, the Jacksons, the Freers, the Brookmans, the Wilsons, the Michelmores, of course, the Minnies, the Heaths, Pat Johnson. Pat Johnson used to live in what is known today as Woodcutter's Cottage in Kuitpo Forest. Pat used to be the bullock driver. I still recall Pat Johnson driving his bullocks around quite close to our house, where the forest boundary was, ploughing fire breaks. I am not sure whether he had six bullocks or four, which was quite a feat in those days. He named all his bullocks. He had Roany. He had Strawberry. He had Darkie. I can't remember the other names.

I only spent one year going to school at Kuitpo. Then I went to the Prospect Hill School. The reason I went to Prospect Hill School was because I would be able to pick up the mail from the Prospect Hill Post Office. There was no mail delivered to the property, so our mail always went to the Prospect Hill Post Office. And that was the reason I think my father decided that it would be better if I went up there, so that I could get the mail going home from school. That school was situated just opposite where the Scout Hall is located today. It was a one-teacher school, with sometimes a helper (seven grades). Some of the teachers that I can recall were Mr Wydrowski, Mr Redden, Miss Kaul, Mr Len Burman, Pam Kimba, June Trenorden and, of course, Miss Galley. She was – what should I say? – she was a person who had her method of doing things. But she was absolutely dedicated to what she did. For example, as we became teenagers, she organised Old Scholars' social events. So the teenagers around the town could still go back to the old school and enjoy social events, which was quite successful actually. It was the only entertainment for young people in the immediate area.

The significant thing that I find about Prospect Hill is that it has always been such a caring place, with caring people in it. The Griggs family, the Harvey family, and the Connor family, the Michelmore family; all those families were very much involved in setting up the community of Prospect Hill. I guess there was that need for community spirit because houses were a long way

Figure 11. Family outing. Dave Sheppard's Dodge ute. Third from left Dave Sheppard, next to Jack Palmer, then Olive Sheppard. Others unidentified. Blackfellows Creek, c. 1929, courtesy Glenys and Graeme Usher.

Figure 12. Harry Palmer, 1 January 1936, courtesy Glenys and Graeme Usher.

away and life would get fairly lonely, wouldn't it? So people that lived within a reasonable horse and cart distance would form communities. That happened throughout the state.

Just on the Harveys: they owned a property where Mr Ron Lochier and his family lived years ago. They built a cottage on the property. Part of that property got sold at some stage by the Harveys or the Lochiers. I am not sure which. It is interesting that my grandmother bought part of that property. That was always known to me as Harveys Scrub. Ironically, later on, I became the owner with my brother of that property called Harveys Scrub. That has since been sold. The Connors, the Milligans, the Nicols. The Nicols' base was in Bull Creek but they did have land that came into Prospect Hill. Later on, Gordon Nicols built a dairy on the land which is now where Lindsay Gibson lives.

On that land at the top of the hill is what they called the 'Parting Tree'. It is a flowering gum that was planted many years ago. As I said, the church was the only building in there and the vestry was where everything was held. When they went out to social functions, the story was that the boys would take their girlfriends home as far as the top of that hill. And vice versa. The tree is where they would part. It is called the 'Parting Tree'.

The Pikes came a bit later on. The Michelmores have always been there. The Oakleys, the Sweetmans, the Maidments, the Mawsons, the Rogers. The Rogers owned a property which is section 53, a property which borders what is now Milligan Road. Tom Dixon, the Sheppards, there were two lots of Rogers, another lot down in what we used to call Tin Town. That's between Prospect Hill and Meadows. Down there were the Connors, I recall, and the Rogers and the Harveys, another family of Harveys. I still remember that Mr Herb Connor used to grow tobacco down there, years ago. Later on, the Gills – they were there many years ago. The Wallaces a little bit later, the Harpers, of course. The very first were the Morrises, which

Figure 13. William J Griggs Playground, Prospect Hill, 13 October, 2020.
Photos: Jiayuan Liang

Daytime.

Nighttime.

is now called Morris' Hill. That was taken up by the Dieners, the Fred Wrights, the Bob Morrises, the Eddie Eckerts, the Cyril Moores, the Kuchels, the Waits, the Longs, the Smarts, the Foggos, the Coads, the Hills, the Hoskings, and later on the Hughes, Palmers, Howards, Zerks. That's some of the names.

Many things happen in Prospect Hill only because everybody pulls together and makes things happen. In those days, we never had such things as government grants, or grants from anywhere else where you could get money. If we wanted to do something in Prospect Hill, then we had to earn it ourselves as a community. And that's what used to happen. As far as community interests and activities go, I guess we go back a far way. I was Trustee of the Meadows Methodist Parsonage Trust for some time. I still remember painting the underground tank there when I was in my late teens with some sort of paint. You had to be careful about the fumes. It was a round tank, mostly set in the ground with a dome top that had an entrance. I had to get out of that tank very, very quickly because I felt myself going into a daze. I thought 'I could become unconscious from the fumes and no-one would find me'.

The other thing I was involved with in my earlier days was the Meadows Agricultural Bureau which involved many Prospect Hill people. After a while I was the Assistant Secretary, and then the Vice President and then the President. I am a life member of that today.

The next thing I was involved with that I can recall was the Prospect Hill Progress Committee, first initiated by Keith Griggs. The Progress Committee was the forerunner of the Prospect Hill Community Centre today. There was an amalgamation of the Progress Committee and the Memorial Hall Committee which was built later and they combined and made the centre as it is known today. I was involved there during the building of the W.J. Griggs Playground Project. I can still remember clearing the trees off that site and it being levelled. William John Griggs was the father of Keith Griggs, Keith John. William Griggs married a Miss Marshall. Her mother was Mrs Les Marshall. Les Marshall

Figure 14. The Boy Scout Association's 1936 Corroboree was held in Belair National Park to celebrate South Australia's centenary of European settlement.

Scout Corroboree at National Park, Belair, 26 December 1936 to 4 January 1937. C.G. Tucker, C.W.L. Noon, H.A. Griffin, W. Goward standing outside a tent, courtesy State Library of South Australia.

Boy Scouts gathered around a tent at Belair camp, Scout Corroboree at National Park, Belair. Courtesy History Trust of South Australia, made available under the Creative Commons CC0 1.0 Universal Public Domain Dedication

was the village blacksmith. Mrs Marshall lived in what is now the museum. I remember being told that Keith Griggs had a chat to Pat Connor and a few others about the idea of setting up the old Marshall home as a museum. That was the beginning of the Prospect Hill Museum that exists today. Later on, the Prospect Hill War Memorial Hall was built.

Another interest was the Prospect Hill Table Tennis Club. I spent some time there as the Captain, the Secretary and the President and I am a life member of that. I was never a member of the Tennis Club, only the Table Tennis Club. My wife (Betty Ann) and my family were members, of course. That tennis court was built by local labour, local people using horse and scoops to level it out. Some of the families involved with that were the Griggs, the Harveys, the Connors, the Pikes, the Milligans and the Lovelocks. Later on they installed electric lighting on the courts. At the time that my wife, Betty Ann, and my children played, I think there were four or five teams in the Prospect Hill Club. Unfortunately, today, there is no club there anymore.

I wasn't involved with this but I remember when the Country Women's Association was there. It was the first hall in the district for social occasions. Prospect Hill had a very active CWA branch, originally a building which was a school down at Mosquito Crek, down near Langhorne Creek. I remember my father and a few other people very much involved in getting that school that was at Mosquito Creek re-erected at Prospect Hill. It was there until Ash Wednesday in 1983. Unfortunately, it got burnt then.

I guess the next thing that I recall is the Prospect Hill Scout Group which was formed in 1944. Keith Griggs was the first leader. We originally met on a Saturday afternoon in the Prospect Hill tennis shed. That was a little shed that was built down on the tennis courts. Later we moved up to the shed belonging to Mr W.J. and Keith Griggs. We used to meet where they kept their car and truck. Every week they would take the vehicles out so we could meet and after we had finished they would put them back again. Later, the Meadow Scout Hall, which was not being used, was transported from Meadows up to Prospect Hill. Originally, that hall was the Post Office of the Belair Corroboree (Jamboree) of 1936. I had a bulldozer in those days and I levelled the site for that scout hall. Keith Griggs gave the land for it and later gave that land to the Scout Association, which still owns the land today. The scout group continues today and in August 2014 there was a celebration of 70 years of scouting in Prospect Hill, non-stop.

Another interest that I was involved in for a while was the Blackfellows Creek CFS, Country Fire Service. Firstly, it was set up before I was involved by locals Bob Morris, Claude Connor, Arch Oakley, and Pat and Pete Connor and I think some other people. My father, as well. To start with, they put a tank with water in it, on Mr Morris' truck or his little utility. Later, the Meadows Council supplied a hand operated pump to go on whoever's vehicle it got put on when it was necessary. Later still, there was a shed built on Mr Arch Oakley's property and that's where the tank used to be housed. While I was involved in that we raised funds and built the extension to the CFS fire shed which became a meeting room, and a shower room, kitchen. I levelled the site for that extension, of course. Also I was involved for a while in the Meadows Valley Camera Club. Several years actually. And that is still going today I believe, which is fantastic. I was also a member of Prospect Hill's Band of Hope at some stage but that is a long time ago. I guess that's mainly my involvement in Prospect Hill.

Figure 15. Mr and Mrs George Tester of Clarendon in a horse-drawn buggy at Prospect Hill, c. 1900, courtesy State Library of South Australia.

Prospect Hill has always been a very, very caring community. It has always taken an interest in historical things, such as the Old Flag Tree. We learned about that a long time ago. The story is that they used to put a flag up the flagpole and send the messages to another flagpole nearer to the coast, and that would then go out to sea. So people in Prospect Hill could get a message of when there was a boat coming in. They would know when to go down and get groceries or whatever stores they needed to get. That is what I have been told. How much of that is absolutely right, I wouldn't know. But I would say it's right.

In those days, of course, they used to go by horse and buggy or wagon down to Adelaide to get supplies. Going all that distance would have taken a day to get there and another day to come back. And so it goes on. The Griggs set up a little shop where the museum and post office are today. That is where the people used to get the groceries the Griggs brought from Adelaide. Another significant spot in Prospect Hill is what we used to call the China Wall. That's situated towards Bull Creek on a property that, when I was growing up, used to belong to Clyde Wait. China Wall is a natural huge, huge rock that resembles a huge wall. It is still there today of course. Old quarries were set up purely to build people's homes. There used to be a stone quarry out on what used to be the Pike property. That's probably the main things that come to my mind about significant places in Prospect Hill and how they managed in the early, early days.

There are places that are important historic sites in the Prospect Hill area. They're all part of the history of the district. These things need to be mentioned otherwise they will be lost forever. There are sites of interest around Prospect Hill and Bull Creek, including what is known today as Bells Cottage. Bells Cottage is in a place we called Bells Gully, which is now all pine forest. My grandmother's brother owned that property back in those days before it was sold to Forestry South Australia. The other item of interest is Blackfellows Creek School. I remember some of the Connors attended that school. The block, which is now forest today, right next to Prospect Hill, used to be known as Maidments Block. They were clearing all the timber off that block and then burning it so they could plant the pines. That block was next to Sweetmans Block, which later became *Donnybrook*, the property of Mr and Mrs Jack and Lil Connor. The original Harvey home was where the Harveys first set up when they came into the district. It is situated on what is now

Hammersmith Road. Previously, the property was owned by the Lochier family. Prior to that, of course, it goes back to the Harveys. Part of that old home is still standing today and is still being used.

Christmas Hill Road goes from Brookman Road up to Blackfellows Creek Road. I have always heard that Christmas Hill Road was named because there were many, many Christmas tree bushes there, which are natives. They are still there today. They were called Christmas tree bushes because they always flower at Christmas time. There were many of them throughout the Adelaide Hills. That's my understanding of how that hill got called Christmas Hill.

Survey Hill was a base for the surveyors when they surveyed the district for the first time. It is located in Prospect Hill, approximately half a kilometre from the post office.

Archie's Bridge is on what is now Black Nursery Road. It is over the first creek that you come to after leaving Brookman Road on the way to Prospect Hill. The story there is that many years ago there was a guy by the name of Archie. Archie had been somewhere and apparently he was coming home. He had had a bit too much alcohol. He probably wasn't clear on what he was doing. He attempted to cross the flooded creek, or a flooded bridge, and he didn't make it. It finished up that he got drowned. So my grandmother, and my uncles, used to talk about Archie's Bridge.

The other one is Wattle Gully. It was called Wattle Gully because there were millions of wattle trees there. The wattle bark industry was a really big industry in the district at that time. There was many, many wattles throughout the district, particularly on the lower ground. The wattle bark was used for tanning leather. They used to cut the wattle into lengths, strip the bark off it, dry the bark out and send it to the tannery. A weighbridge was set up at Echunga. It would weigh the wattle bark before it got to the tannery, so people knew how much tonnage they had. People were paid according to the tonnage of the wattle bark. The people at the weighbridge would get the wattle bark to wherever it needed to go. That was quite a major industry in the Adelaide hills. Of course, it is not there today. The wattle being a native, you wouldn't be allowed to harvest it today, which is probably a good thing.

Another interesting site is the Blackwood Gully gold diggings. There were only one or two mines. There is only one that is obvious today. That is over on the property called 'Harewood' which was owned by Sir Douglas Mawson. They didn't find a whole lot of gold there so they didn't continue. The old mine is still there. There were quite a few gold diggings at Blackfellows Creek, which is south of where Kuitpo Colony was located. The buildings are there today. There is an interesting story I heard about that, and it's true, because if you go there you can find the evidence. It was quite a busy gold mine at one stage. They built a huge dam in Blackfellows Creek to get water for their gold panning. They built it with flood gates in it, so they could open up the flood gates when they got a flood and let the water through. They could close it and build up the water reserve level. I believe it was the first winter after they built it. This story concerned the person who had the responsibility of opening those flood gates at the appropriate time. Here, again, the story is that he got on the alcohol a little bit too much and he forgot about opening the flood gates. The result was that they lost the dam and the whole lot went. It has never been re-built. If you go there it is hard to see it now, because it is very, very densely covered in scrub. But I can still remember where you could see the evidence of the bank, where it left the roadside and where it crossed the other side of the hill.

There is another mine down there, further down from the dam, right beside a hill. There is a spring in that mine, which is about halfway up the hill. When they set up Kuitpo Colony, they had a pipe running from that spring right up the Colony to provide water all year round. The spring actually stopped the mine from operating because there was too much water. That spring is still running today.

There was a mine with building stone on 'Woodlands' which is the former Pike property. That was really good building stone. All the stone in the Pike homestead that Gerland Pike built came out of that mine. I believe that's where the stone came from, for other houses around the district. Also, there was a talc mine, on Stone's property down Mt Magnificent way. While I have never actually seen that mine I have seen the talc that was produced from it. I am not really sure whether it was actually commercialised.

Another industry was sawmilling. There were two sawmills. One was on Sir Douglas Mawson's property on Wickam Hill Road. I certainly do remember that one functioning. For many, many years there was a huge heap of sawdust there. Actually, I carted some of that sawdust away, as time went on, for other people. Much of it went over to Wistow way for a man who was setting up a blueberry farm. Apparently, sawdust was what he wanted to get the soil right for his blueberry farm. I have never been back to see if the blueberries were successful or not. I would be interested to know.

The other sawmill was on Brookman Road. I don't know who owned that property when the mill was built. I do know that my uncle Archie Michelmore owned that property after whoever owned it in the first place. I have got a feeling that the original owner might have been Sir Douglas Mawson, but I am not sure about that. That mill operated as quite an industrious mill until there was a fire. It got burnt when there was a bushfire in 1929. That was the end of that.

I remember my mother telling me about the 1929 bushfire, years and years ago. I didn't see it. I was only a baby then. I can remember some of the old waste timber around there. The 1929 fire went up through the district, through the block opposite the farm at Prospect Hill where we used to live at *Sunnybrae*. I remember my mother telling me about the fire, on property which is now owned by Forestry South Australia.

There used to be a fire lookout tower on what is now Harvey Road. It was towards the Forestry Department office. It was on the hill just behind the office, actually. The Forester would go up there frequently when there was danger of a bushfire. He used to ride his horse up from where the Forestry headquarters are today. Des Derwood lived at the Forestry headquarters initially, and after that Mr Chalk. They used to go up there every so often and have a look around the district. If they saw smoke they would immediately take action.

Unfortunately, that tower has been demolished, which is a pity. We had a photo of that tower. At this point, I haven't been able to find it. I am still trying to find it and I have spoken to my sister, because I think she might have one, too. I can remember as kids we used to go up there with my grandmother. It wasn't used as a fire tower then. We'd climb up that tower, which was a great place to get a good view. There is nothing there at this stage. Now, of course, National Parks have got control of it. I believe that there should be a plaque put up where that tower was, with a short description about it. Otherwise, all these things are just lost forever. To me, they're all part of the history of the district.

Before the European settlement of Prospect Hill, say during the Aboriginal settlement of the area, there is only two things that comes to my mind. One was about the Rogers, who lived up on section 53 at Prospect Hill, which later became the Milligans' property. This particular part became Colin Milligans' property. I remember Max Milligan telling me that he remembers being told of the people that used to live down there. The Aborigines, or some of the Aborigines, used to go down there and ask for 'baccie'. One of the things the Aborigines were most impressed with was seeing the steam coming out of the kettle. They found that extremely fascinating. That is one story that I have heard.

The other story I heard was from some of the older residents around Prospect Hill. They remember when there were Aborigines camping down in the Blackfellows Creek area, which is south of Prospect Hill, and leads into Kuitpo Colony. I would think that Blackfellows Creek is named in reference to Aboriginal people. I have never been told. I have never tried to find out either, to be quite frank. But I would think that would be fairly obvious. Incidentally, whilst there was never an identifiable community there, there were people who lived there, like a few of the names I have mentioned: the Connors, Oakleys, Stones. They were the main ones, way back.

Blackfellows Creek is still identified by the Country Fire Service (CFS) Station. It is still known as the Blackfellows Creek Country Fire Service. So that name will stick in that area. Of course, Blackfellows Creek itself flowed in a southerly direction down towards, and connected up with, what is now known as the Finniss River.

On the day of the Ash Wednesday bushfires, I was driving one of the CFS trucks. We were out in Kuitpo Forest, next to

Blackfellows Creek, because we had a fire there the day before. We were out there that Ash Wednesday, that morning, putting out smouldering tree stumps. While we were on the job, we got a message to say that a fire had started at McLaren Flat. Of course, that fire became the great fire – that Ash Wednesday fire we all know of. Unfortunately, that fire was heading south from McLaren Flat, or a bit east perhaps. Then a south wind came up. That gave it a huge fire front that just blew it straight up into Kuitpo Forest, Prospect Hill, Ashbourne and all those areas. Terrific fire. Horrific fire.

That afternoon we drove down to give some assistance at Hope Forest. That's where the fire had got to at that time. Then the message was given that we should go back home, which we did. I still remember going speedily back up to the Blackfellows Creek (CFS) fire shed. That's where we were stationed. There was a team of about six of us. Graeme Usher was there and so was Tom Sadler. Then we realised that it was really getting up, coming up our way. So it was a matter of everybody fend for themselves. I raced off home because we were a bit further down Norris' Creek. It just so happened that I owned the property next to the fire shed. On the way home I opened up all the gates through the paddocks so that stock could go through from paddock to paddock and not get caught by the fire.

When I arrived home the fire hadn't reached there at that stage. My two sons, Andrew and Stephen, were there. It wasn't long before the fire did get to our house because it wasn't any more than 100 metres from the forest. So we copped it good and proper. My sons already had the tank and the trailer down there and got everything ready.

It was a day that I will never forget. It was an absolute fluke that we saved the house. The three of us had been putting out spot fires all afternoon. We were absolutely exhausted. We sat on a bank at the side of the road just to get our energy back again. At that stage we thought that the fires had burnt some old cars that were outside the sheds. We started to walk that way. I looked back at the house and the fire had got into the ivy that was growing on the walls of the house. We raced back. As providence would have it, we had previously placed half a bucket of water near the ivy. The placement was accidental. The ivy was on fire and the fire was about one foot below the guttering. If it had got there, that would have been the end of the house. We threw the water onto the ivy. I grabbed the ivy and pulled it down. Another half a minute and it would have been too late.

That we were able to keep fighting the fire was due to the strength and determination of all three of us, Andrew, Stephen and myself, the ability of the human body to somehow find extreme energy in a crisis so we could keep going. Between the house and the forest, we had a small paddock where my daughters, Ann-Marie and Heather, kept their horses. The horse manure was catching alight and blowing down to where we had a strip of garden along the house. Luckily, we had a bit of a gravel track through there, that helped heaps. But we had to keep putting spot fires out to save the house.

When we were desperately trying to save the house, my wife and daughters got in the car and went to the Meadows Oval. My two sons had told them to do that. I wasn't home at that point. My wife, Betty, told me later that a message came through to Meadows Oval that a house had been burnt. Betty was standing next to the people who owned that house. The first thing the husband said to his wife was, "Did you save my guitar?" Well, she did. She took the guitar with her.

That night, Betty and the family did not know if they had a house to go to. So one of the teenager's friends (Bucko) rode his motorbike from Meadows to check whether the house was still there. He was able to ride back and tell Betty that it was still there, so that was a huge relief. But we lost sheds and a lot of other things. That morning we had something like 7,000 square bales of hay stored; that night we had nothing. I said we had none, it was smouldering. We had none that was useful. But thanks to the generosity of many kind people, they gave us some hay to get us through for a few days until we got ourselves organised. We lost many kilometres of fencing, as did many other people, but at least we were able to save our house. Ash Wednesday affected the whole district and a large, large number of people. Unfortunately, there were seven houses burnt in the area and there were two deaths, which was tragic.

The old Prospect Hill School got burnt. At that stage it was used as a residence. Incidentally, the people that lived in that house at the time had already had their house destroyed in the Darwin Cyclone. They come down this way and they lived at Prospect Hill and they lost their house again, at Prospect Hill. It's not just someone's house. It's all the contents, their memories, the things that they cherished. It is tragic, and you can't do anything about it.

It is absolutely a miracle how the museum didn't get destroyed. There was a little bit of timber that got scorched, badly scorched. It even got charred a bit. There was a building next door to where the museum is today. The museum didn't get burnt because it had a stone building next to it, between the sheds and the museum and the Marshall home. That was made of stone, that was the only reason the museum didn't get burnt. All the sheds that belonged to the Griggs' from that

Figure 16. Prospect Hill Primary School after the Ash Wednesday bushfire, courtesy Glenys and Graeme Usher.

building, further up towards their old dairy that is a little way up the hill, they all got destroyed. The stone building next to the museum was rebuilt. There was part of the wall still standing but everything else had to be cleared away. We were lucky to get a very good stone mason. He did an excellent job rebuilding.

Prospect Hill has always been a community that has worked well together. I guess the thing that stands out most of all to me in relation to the after-effects of the bushfire is the way that the catastrophe pulled everybody together to a much greater degree. Just after Ash Wednesday, Malcolm Slade and a few other people organised what was basically a wake. I think pretty well everybody in Prospect Hill turned out that night. It was held on the tennis courts. I guess one of the good things that has come out of it – and the realities in life – is that something good can come out of something bad.

The Memorial Hall didn't get burned, thank goodness. The hall became a depot for relief purposes and donations of clothing and whatever. That was the depot and a base for Jean Harvey, whose house was burnt down. She lived in the hall for quite some time, until they could arrange to get accommodation back where their house was, which wasn't that far from Prospect Hill. There was a fundraising effort arranged by some locals to raise money to help the people who lost their homes in Ash Wednesday. Despite the fact that the fundraisers had losses, they hadn't lost their homes. So they banded together an amateur hour to raise funds for the people who did lose property. Because the Scout Hall and the CWA rooms had been destroyed, the community immediately took action. Due to a lot of help from service clubs, particularly, the Scout Hall was rebuilt. And I know that there were scout groups that gave money towards the building of the Prospect Hill Scout Hall. I know that because I was involved from day one and I have been involved up until a couple of years ago. I levelled the site for the new community hall, which is built on the old CWA site, the same site, after Ash Wednesday. I also built the dam on the Community Association property, down below the tennis courts. I ripped the trenches for planting the trees on the community property on the southern side that was planted after Ash Wednesday. The Scout Hall was also destroyed, but there was a new hall built around 12 months later.

Part of the heritage property now is the old schoolhouse that was the school building at Meadows. It got moved down by the Education Department to their museum at Morphett Vale.

Figure 17. Meadows one-room school, opened 1893, now relocated to Prospect Hill Museum, courtesy Claire Smith.

It sat there for quite a while. They then decided to disband that museum. Luckily, very luckily, we got to know about it. Prospect Hill people made arrangements and we were able to get that hall back again into the district. As far as I know, the Meadows people were very comfortable about it, moving the Meadows School back to the Prospect Hill Museum. That was quite a major task because it is quite a sizeable building. It is very, very, very tall. It was my son and I that organised bringing that building back to Prospect Hill. We hired a low loader, which was driven by my son, John. Transporting the building to Prospect Hill meant contacting the police, the Electricity Trust of South Australia and so on, having to lift power lines and all sorts of things, but it happened. I was the one who carted the rubble and who levelled out the site to sit the building on. When the building got there, it was in pretty bad repair. I still remember painting the roof of the darn thing. It is a long way from the roof to the ground. It has a really steep gable roof. I had a rope tied around me anchored to the opposite side, so if I slipped I wouldn't fall off the roof. I was glad that rope was there a couple of times, I can tell you.

Later on, the CWA room was replaced in the form of a hall. The reason that got built reasonably early in the piece was that the Wollongong Council from New South Wales collected money for the South Australian bushfire relief. Geoff Simpson was the mayor, or chairman, of our local council at that time. He suggested that that money go to Prospect Hill. So that was the biggest part of the cost and made the new building possible. There were other monies put into it. Of course, there were other monies put into the Scout Hall besides the funds that came from the service clubs and Wollongong Council. This is another example of people pulling together, and people helping people in the times of distress. Let's hope that people help people at all times, but when the chips are down, that is when the best of people come out and that was very much proved on Ash Wednesday.

One of the good things that came out of the bushfire was that the water system has been improved. Before the bushfire, everybody that lived in the district used to clean up all the leaves, the gutters, the grass. I know that the Griggs certainly did. People would generally clean up before the summer. So if there was a fire, at least we had a better chance of doing something with it. Because in front of the Prospect Hill Museum there is a road. It is a T-junction. There is quite a lot of roadway there which obviously helped save the house where Keith used to live. That road would have saved that house without a doubt. The roads don't stop sparks, but they certainly stop the running fire. It's interesting what a small patch of bare ground will do, how it breaks the speed of a fire. We found that on our own property. We lost a lot of fences. But the fences next to the firebreaks on the southern side, those posts or any pine posts were still there. Any red gum posts went, but there were still some in other places. The heat was that fierce it actually burnt the pine posts. They say that they don't burn, but when it gets hot enough they do.

Following Ash Wednesday, there was a community drive – all in again – to build a water system. We built the large concrete tank up on the hill nearby, next to Flag Tree Reserve. We put in a water system. We put in a pump and underground piping to take water. And we put sprinklers on the roof of what is now the museum. We did that to be able to hopefully never let it happen again. We have water there and sprinklers on site. We had none of that on Ash Wednesday, of course. So it was tragic. The new water system is something that is good that came out of it.

What the bushfire has done – all the loss and the tragedy and all the homes, also the two lives that were lost – has made Prospect Hill a far better known community within the whole state. Before Ash Wednesday, it was a quiet little town, well known within a certain circle. But probably not much known outside of that area. Since Ash Wednesday, and everything that has happened since, Prospect Hill became far better known as an example of rebuilding a community.

One big thing that stands out as to the effects of Ash Wednesday is people helping people, and people that weren't affected by Ash Wednesday helping those that were. It was fantastic. Fantastic. Destruction, rebuild, community spirit and the fire protection system that was put in which is still there today. The big thing that stands out in it all was people helping people, from all over the state and interstate as well.

Prospect Hill today is still a very close-knit community. But I think I would be right in saying the whole community is perhaps not as closely knit as it was many, many years ago. That's probably because it has got bigger. More properties have been built on. More houses have been built. Years ago, families inter-married and so everybody knew everybody. Right this day as we speak I think there is only one member of the Griggs family, Bev Griggs, left living in Prospect Hill. However, there are three Griggs still living in Meadows: Mervin, Phil and Trevor. The Harvey family lived at Prospect Hill until just recently, but they've pretty well all gone now. The Michelmore family, there's only one in Prospect Hill, that's Chris. The Connors, well there's different Connors. The Lovelocks, I'll say they are descendants of the Connor family. That's the main families that are still represented. There's been a big change actually.

Nowadays, people have come to live in Prospect Hill from outside the community. They moved to Prospect Hill because they wanted to. And I can understand that, because it is a great place to live. Of course it is. It has fantastic views. They can have an outdoor country lifestyle. Once it took a day to get from Prospect Hill to Adelaide. Today is only takes an hour. This means that people who would once have lived in Adelaide can now live in Prospect Hill. Some of those people certainly become very much involved in the community. Some not as much. That's understandable. They are working. They have got long distances to travel. There are many reasons that some community residents don't get as involved as much as others. But there are quite a few others, many others, that have come

BUYING BOOKS

The Advertiser

BUSHFIRE PICTURES: P.16/17

# 18 DIE IN STATE'S DAY OF DISASTER

ALP offers tax cuts, more jobs

MOMENT BY MOMENT . . .

Act allows police chief wide power

Why? A tragic question without answer

$13\frac{1}{2}$% p.a.

...that's got to be Beneficial.

Beneficial

Luxury Demos to go!

Fairmont Ghia SAVE $2198

GL Meteor SAVE $1543

Laser Ghia SAVE $910

Fairlane SAVE $2288

Fairway Ford

Figure 18. Eighteen die in State's Day of Disaster, *Advertiser*, Thursday 17 February 1983 page 1.

into the community and they do get involved. And that will, if it is all done in the right spirit, continue to grow Prospect Hill.

Some people have moved from Prospect Hill to other areas. For example, I now live in Encounter Bay, near Victor Harbour. People move around today in a way they weren't able to do in the distant past. Rather than harnessing a horse and buggy, today people can just hop in a car. I think this mobility has affected the cohesion of some communities, but Prospect Hill still has a strong community spirit. Even though some of the residents of Prospect Hill now live in different places, we are still in touch with each other. There is a strong bond. One of the reasons for that bond is that we have an annual reunion each year in the community centre. That wouldn't happen if somebody within the community didn't make it happen. Each year, somebody does.

I think Prospect Hill has a great future. I think the Prospect Hill museum has a great future. It was Keith Griggs' dream and vision that it would become an active museum – located in the stone building that was rebuilt, next to the museum as it is today. At that stage, we also built in there a little kitchen area, with a sink. The thinking was that it could be opened up. The committee, or the people responsible, could serve afternoon tea and scones and all of that sort of thing. I don't think that has happened very much at this stage, but the point is that it is there. It's built for the future.

Prospect Hill is my home and always will be. I've got a son up there. I still go back up there frequently to the scout group, very frequently over the last several years. Looking ahead, I believe for the community centre as a whole to move forward, which includes the museum, it would be prudent to consider setting up a five-year-plan as to where they want to go, what they want to do in the next five years and how they can improve. Then they should review that plan every twelve months, tick off the things they have done and deal with the things they haven't done, in order of priority. They should do whatever they can to pull the whole community together and create interest within the community. That way it gives more support and the community can continue to prosper. I believe that there is great potential there. But it is not going to happen unless people get involved. Unfortunately, as happens in many things throughout the state, all too often the chores get left to a few. Eventually those few burn out. That is when things start to go backwards. I think Prospect Hill needs to make very sure that they don't allow that to happen by doing whatever it takes to pull the community together and keep the interest there and keep improving things. Because the fact is success breeds success. If the community can see an active group in there driving that, and doing things, they will do even more than they do now. They do heaps now mind you. I think it is a credit to them.

Since we left there's been some big improvements. The more people see those successful things, the more likely they are to want to get on board. I really think that is what the community will need to aim for. As I said before, I believe there is a great future there if it can be administered in the best possible way, and driven by enthusiasm. I've got to admit that one doesn't normally ponder on the many situations that have happened in a lifetime. Well, not a lifetime yet, I hope. But up till now, put it that way.

The changes I have seen in my lifetime in the Prospect Hill area, and life in general, are tremendous. My mind boggles. Because changes are happening quicker, my mind boggles as to where it is all going to be in the next fifty years. I would like to think that the Prospect Hill Museum will be a very, very thriving enterprise in the Prospect Hill area forever. But to make that happen, we have got to keep younger people in the system.

Because what happens, when you have many older people, organisations and museums die because there are no younger people to keep it up. So that's another priority: keep younger people involved and do whatever it takes to encourage them.

# Raymond John Bailey

My parents and I came to the Prospect Hill area in 1945 after my father got out of the army. He took a position at Kuitpo Colony as Probation Officer to look after some of the more unfortunate people from around Adelaide. Eventually, my brother and my sisters were born up here. Our first home was a wattle and daub house on Cyril Moore's property. Later on, a house was built for us on the Kuitpo Colony property. Probably it would not be built today as it was then as the walls were made of large sheets of asbestos since other materials were in short supply due to the war. That was about 1948. Regrettably, this house was destroyed in the fire.

In those early times, I was simply a student here going to the Prospect Hill school. Along with the others, I suppose in those early times, I just had a good time here. My parents were involved with the community, doing the new tennis courts. They were members of the Prospect Hill tennis club, which was very active at the time. Thinking back fifty-odd years ago, there was tremendous involvement with the community. The one thing that I can recall: the building of the new tennis courts, which are behind the old tennis courts. I can remember working bees to

Figure 19. Ray Bailey, 18 November, 2014. Photo: Antoinette Hennessy.

do some concreting up there. As kids, we travelled all through the district having a very good time with the other kids from various tennis clubs: Meadows, Kangarilla, Flaxley, Bull Creek. My parents became involved with square dancing, and I can remember that they used to have square dance classes in our home back in the fifties. And there were a lot of people that joined in those classes, and then went with my parents down to Adelaide for some of the other square dances that were on at that stage. I moved away in about 1955 when I started going to high school, and I was boarding in Adelaide. It wasn't until 2009, 2010 when I became involved again. Between those times, I came back to the community.

I can recall coming back here after the fire, there was a community get-together here, I suppose, to raise funds. And sometimes I would drive through the area and if I happened to see Keith Griggs around, I would stop and say g'day. And a couple of times, over Easter periods, I would come up and look around and go through the museum. But it wasn't until 2009, 2010, when I became involved again with the community, this time with the museum. I've become involved with restorations at the museum, and I'm usually here every Sunday and occasionally at odd days during the week. I restore virtually anything that is made out of steel: engines, old ploughs, grain crushers, chaff cutters, *et cetera*. But I don't like seeing anything that is old destroyed, because I think if we don't do it now, then the people coming up – our children's children – will have no idea of what our forefathers did. And that's important to know.

Regrettably, I don't know much about the Aboriginal history of the area, except we had a belief that the Aboriginals were moving between this area, Meadows – they would go down along Blackfellows Creek through Kuitpo Colony, and then on down towards Mount Compass and Encounter Bay. I was told this around 1950, when I was about eight years old, by one of the miners from the Mount Monster mine, which closed around 1900 after the dam burst. He was well in his seventies at the time, and I think he was talking about the 1890s. That's the only thing that I can recall about the Aboriginals. But I believe that in various

Figure 20. Bailey house. Photo by Joan Bailey, c. 1950.
Courtesy Rod and Ray Bailey and families.

parts of the hills here, there were mounds of seashells found, so obviously they were bringing some shells with them, probably mussels *et cetera* to eat on the way.

The early days of European settlement in Prospect Hill would have been very, very tough. You know, to clear the scrub. If you drive down Milligan Road now you can see the remnants of the scrub that the settlers were facing. They had to clear it. And they had to provide food for the families as well, so to go out, cut down trees, grub out roots, build fences – and at the same time, try and find something for their family to eat at night, or during the day. It would have been very, very tough.

Kuitpo Colony was originally founded by the Reverend Samuel Forsythe who started to establish it around about 1927, at the beginning of the Depression Era. It was established so people who were down on their luck and feeling pretty hopeless could go there and get work, and get a sense of belonging to a community. It was more or less carved out of the bush: they built three separate camps there – number one, two, three, and eventually number four, but number four was a sister, a collection of railway carriages deep into the scrub. And they used to raise chooks down there, and the eggs would be taken to Adelaide every week in the truck.

When my father went there in 1945, he was the probation officer, so that he was responsible for the minor court offenders, bearing in mind in this era, public drunkenness was a gaolable offence. And rather than fill up Yatala, or even Kyeema with drunks, they would send them to Kuitpo where they were not allowed to have any alcohol. And my father was then responsible for them to serve out the period that they were sent there by the courts, but it wasn't a gaol. They were allowed to go to Adelaide weekly – not every week, but people would go down to Adelaide on the truck on Fridays. They had to be back at the central mission, which was next to 5KA by the time the truck went. The truck would not wait for them. So if they missed it, then they had to get on the Meadows bus, come back up to Meadows, and then walk from Meadows back to Kuitpo, which was around about ten miles.

Eventually, in the late forties, they established a pottery there and initially produced agricultural pipes, and then as there was a huge demand for flowerpots from the nurseries, they started producing flower pots from 50 mm up to around about 250 mm in diameter. And they would take a load of flowerpots to Adelaide maybe once or twice a week. But the injection moulding of plastics finished that in the fifties. The Reverend Neil Usher was the manager of Kuitpo Colony; he had the main connections between the colony and the people in Adelaide, the Reverend Samuel Forsythe. There are other people down in that area: Jim

Figure 21. Photo of Sarah McHarg's niece, Sarah Elizabeth McHarg, taken at Liverpool, England in 1864, courtesy Prospect Hill Museum.

Clooney ran the dairy at Kuitpo Colony, and he was the one that started the engines up about 4 o'clock in the morning to produce the power for the colony and the milking; Bernie Wenham, a timber cutter and farmer. And I suppose Cyril Moore of where we originally stayed on his property – he was a dairy farmer; and, of course, the Oakleys, dairy farmers that lived about half a kilometre from where we had our house on Cyril Moore's property. Pat Connor, who was another name – dairy farmer down towards Blackfellows Creek. But there are many others that, whilst I didn't know them, we knew them as names, we knew them to say, 'G'day, Mr Palmer' or 'Hello, Mr Coad', *et cetera*.

By the way, Blackfellows Creek was not named after Aboriginal people. It was named after an American Negro named Jackson who lived along that part of the creek. I am told that he is buried in the Meadows cemetery.

The most important figure of Prospect Hill would be Keith Griggs. He ran the post office, and he had the telephone exchange there. He also was a dairy farmer and he taught music. And he taught me for a number of years, but I probably didn't appreciate it very much.

One of the things that I can recall as a student were the stories of Sarah McHarg. I thought some of these were fanciful. As kids, we had ideas that Sarah was either taken by bushrangers or Aboriginals, but it wasn't until 2009 that I learned part of the truth about what happened to Sarah. And because of that, I became much more involved in looking into the McHarg story. The McHargs came from a little place in Scotland in the parish of Inch, which is very close to the border of England. And they came out in 1839, arrived in Adelaide around about December of 1839. John McHarg brought his family up to what eventually became known as Prospect Hill and settled in a little valley behind the museum. The hill where we now have our engine house was known as McHarg Hill.

In 1841 the Governor-Surveyor, Henry Burr, came into the area with his team of surveyors and his wife, and started surveying. The McHargs who had no title to the land that they were settled on, or they had built their camp on, moved out to a place which eventually became known as McHarg's Creek. Mrs Burr didn't like being left alone because of the Aboriginals that were wandering around the district at the time, and it was arranged for Sarah, who was working for a Mrs Boach in Hindley Street, to come back to her parents' camp, and whenever Mrs Burr was going to be left alone, it was arranged for Sarah to come across and spend time with her. Now the distance between the two camps was only about five kilometres, but she was escorted through the scrub. But one day, Sarah, for some reason, decided she wanted to go back to her parents' camp and left the camp on 3 June, 1841, and she simply disappeared. Her remains were not found for some two years at Currency Creek, and it was a very sad business because she had built herself a little wurley, she made a bed out of reeds, and she had left a message to her mother and her sister. I cannot recall all the words, but one was more or less her last will and testament where she had asked that her effects be left to, originally to her mother, but then to one of her sisters. And it is said that she left a message to one of her sisters: 'Grieve not for me, as I am resigned to my fate.'

Other stories I can recall are of the Flagtree and the Block. To me, the story of the Flagtree, or what we knew of the Flagtree, I found that very interesting. For those that don't know, the Flagtree was a large tree which had, as far as I can ascertain, a flagpole on the top of it to make it look a bit higher, from which a Semaphore system would operate to alert the various settlers of the district of the movement of ships. This line of communication extended from Adelaide right through to Encounter Bay or Victor Harbour. So if ships were seen leaving Adelaide, flags would be run up to notify people, but if ships were seen coming through the backstairs passage, or through the west and turning into the gulf, a system of flags would again go up to alert the travellers, or to alert the farmers that a new ship was heading into Port Adelaide.

And the other item that I mentioned is the Block. Now, the Block is a large block of wood that sits out from the original shop here in Prospect Hill, and the shopkeeper, Mr Griggs, would leave various items that people wanted on this block to be picked up either by a traveller going through or by the people that wanted the goods. But if it was a traveller, he would stop by and see that the parcel was for a Mrs Jones, or Mr Shepherd, or Mr Palmer or someone like that, and he'd think, 'Well, I'm going down past there, I'll take it with me.' And it's a system which would be wonderful to have today, but I'm sure it wouldn't get to the recipients.

One of the most important aspects of Prospect Hill's history is the Ash Wednesday bushfires. I was in Adelaide at a meeting discussing progress with sales. Various phone calls started coming into that office by worried wives, and gradually, the meeting became lessened as people excused themselves and said 'I've got to go home'. Eventually, my wife rang to say, 'Can you come home?'. By this time, when I left Adelaide, I couldn't get up the freeway. The police stopped me from going up the freeway, and I believe my wife, when she left, was one of the last cars that actually got up the freeway.

Our house was located about seven kilometres out from Mount Barker, out towards the summit. I had to go up through Blackwood and Upper Sturt, and I can recall driving up the Upper Sturt Road,

# THE SOUTHERN ARGUS

The Southern Argus, Thursday February 24th, 1983

Vol. 118 No. 6248

PRICE PER COPY 20c.

# HOLOCAUST WEDNESDAY

**Wednesday, 16th February, was a day Australia will never forget. It was a day even the sun was reluctant to welcome. There was still a twilight about at 7.30 a.m., as though the dawn was late. The air was silent, not even the magpies were warbling and in a dam beside the Paris Creek Road four large brown snakes were swimming about as if they too knew danger awaited the day.**

Then the hot wind started and the whole area was filled with dust as paddock after paddock joined in a Mad Hatter's Garden Party with the top soil changing ownership.

At noon fire sirens went in all parts of the State, within an hour the sun was again blood red when great columns of smoke, fanned by the relentless winds, filled the skies.

Kuitpo was alight again, Wickhams Hill was turning from drought brown to burnt black. The South East, Clare Valley and Adelaide Hills were all ablaze.

Locally men and women mobilized with military discipline.

The C.F.S. personnel had the trucks out and into the fire area within minutes of the outbreaks.

In the Strathalbyn area they had already fought one fire in the morning, when flames burnt dry growth in the small copse on the Callington Road opposite the pologrounds.

Meadows became a centre of operations for the McLaren Flat/Kuitpo fire.

C.F.S. units from far and wide were passing through throughout the afternoon. At 5.30 p.m. the order came through that Meadows had to be evacuated, everyone was ordered onto the Oval.

Refugees from McLaren Flat, local residents and passing traffic gathered on the Oval in cars, on horseback, on bicycles. Pets of every kind joined the dozens of frightened people who could see nothing because of the low ceiling of smoke.

All they could do was wait and pray.

## SEA OF FLAME

From Kuitpo the flames rushed down the gullies to Ashbourne.

Looking from above, it was described as a sea of flame, rolling in waves like scarlet liquid. In its path it took everything.

It was not until it had devoured all it could and raced on, that those in it were able to comprehend its horror.

There are many tales of bravery, enough to fill a volume, but in the aftermath have come the stories of heartbreak too.

The young couple who died at Prospect Hill who were caretaking for their friends who had gone on their honeymoon.

The teenage girl who went to look at her horse to see if he was alright and found him blind, his eyes burnt opaque hanging from the sockets.

The woman who had been cutting sandwiches for the firefighters at Prospect Hill when she was told the fire was heading her way.

From nowhere came aid to remove what could be rescued.

Then, as she stood with her 40 dairy cows in the middle of the paddock, the fire on every side, she watched her home explode into flame.

In spite of the heat and their natural fear, the cows stayed with her and were saved.

Then there is the Archer family who lost everything in the Darwin Disaster. On Wednesday they were again wiped out, except for their two donkeys.

## FIRE BLACKENS PROSPECT HILL

In 1973 the small country township of Prospect Hill, near Meadows celebrated their centenary. The two meaningful lines on the front cover of their centenary book were 'From golden days to fields of green', but after last Wednesday's bush fire the fields are charred BLACK.

During Wednesday February 16th, fire left much ruin in the small country town of Prospect Hill.

Some of the historic buildings of the town are now heaps of burned iron and others, though still standing are burned out ruins. The whole countryside shows vividly the aftermath of Ash Wednesday's fire.

C.W.A. branch was formed at Prospect Hill in April 1947. In 1948 a 'Grandmothers' competition' and potato growing added sufficiently to their building fund to enable them in 1948 to buy the soon-to-be-demolished Mines Flat school. This was pulled down, transported to Prospect Hill, erected and added on to and until last Wednesday was a very functional building in the community. All that now stands is the fireplace and chimney, the rest, burned and twisted corrugated iron is nearby on the ground.

Across the road the Prospect Hill Post Office, now used as a museum and the residence next door of Mr. Keith Griggs, though damaged slightly, were saved. Along side the Post Office building the shed housing more museum property was burned to the ground. This building housed farm and blacksmith equipment along with many other interesting relics of the past.

The old primary school and house, built around 1877 by Mrs. Elizabeth Spencer (nee Griggs) and extended in 1914 and again in 1940 to house the expanding number of pupils is now also in ruin. The building, mostly of stone was closed as a school in February

Cont. on page 8

Fire damaged scrub at McHarg's Creek, near Prospect Hill.

FIRST TIME IN HISTORY

## Dust Causes Strathalbyn Races to be Abandoned

The ferocity of the gusty winds on February 16th Ash Wednesday (second), eventually brought about the abandoning of the Strathalbyn Races, after only three races on the nine race program were completed.

## Strath. Council Depot for Fire Appeal

The Strathalbyn District Council office is an official depot for the collection of donations of money for the Bushfire Appeal.

An official receipt will be given.

All donations over $2 are tax deductible.

Part of the Prospect Hill Museum and Keith Griggs' shed.

Figure 22(a). Holocaust Wednesday, *Southern Argus*, Thursday 24 February 1983, p. 1

# HOLOCAUST WEDNESDAY

1979 and has been used as a residence since, most recently by the Archer family.

Scouting has been a mobile occupation for boys at Prospect Hill since 1944 but only in more recent years have they had their own building. This too has been burned to the ground.

Around a dozen houses were destroyed at Prospect Hill in Ash Wednesday's fire along with the deaths of two people and countless numbers of stock and loss of property.

**DANGER NOT YET OVER**

The Kuitpo Forest reeks of death. Since early Thursday morning teams have been working almost nonstop gathering the charred remains of 2,500 sheep, 416 cattle, 30 horses, 225 poultry, five goats and countless wild creatures.

Great pits 100 ft. long, 10 ft. deep and 20 ft. wide have been dug and filled. The job seems endless, the smell appalling, but still they work on.

Veterinary surgeons were here, there and everywhere, trying to save animals where they could and ending the agony of those beyond hope.

Sleep has become almost a stranger for the C.F.S. personnel. The Meadows units have been on constant duty since Monday 14th, and throughout the Strathalbyn and Meadows District Council areas the units have been on mopping up operations since Wednesday, working night and day.

Until rain comes this vigilance will have to continue because another day of hot winds like Wednesday could see a repeat of the holocaust.

Stumps are still burning deep in the earth and spot fires are still occurring.

A total of 25,000 hectares and 190 properties were affected by the Kuitpo / McLaren Flat / Meadows / Ashbourne / Paris Creek blaze.

Relief Centres have been set up in major towns. Service Club men have been helping replace fences and tonnes of clothing and bedding have been donated.

The Red Cross, C.F.S. Auxiliaries, C.W.A. all have been working to give aid in what ever field they can.

**WILL WE REMEMBER?**

There is no doubt the holocaust will always be remembered but what of the other fire victims of this summer?

The Wistow fire only three months ago has already become history and yet to its victims the horror was as bad, their feed losses as real and yet still they wait for insurance payouts and assistance with fencing.

Once the drama is over we all tend to forget that the farmer must go on, his cows still need feeding and milking and his other stock still need fodder.

## MACCLESFIELD FIRE THURSDAY

A fire broke out in Macclesfield last Thursday morning between the back of Joylinda Stud and the Cemetery.

Fortunately it was brought under control before it had spread too far, travelling within six inches of the fence line but not burning a single post.

## SPECIAL BUSHFIRE RELIEF TEAM

It was announced on Tuesday that a special team of Bushfire Relief workers is being appointed to help the fire victims deal with their grief and shock.

Following Cabinet's decision to recruit 30 special workers to help fire victims the Department for Community Welfare is appointing them this week and they will begin work immediately.

It is expected the full team will be available to victims in the South East, Adelaide Hills and Clare from next week.

The appointments will be for up to six months depending on the needs of the victims in each bushfire area.

The team is to be specially selected from local communities and will be involved in social work and dealing with family crises and other problems.

They will be specially trained to make sure they are fully informed on all benefits and services available for bushfire victims.

The people affected by the fire will have access through those Bushfire Relief workers to the Chairman of the State Government Bushfire Relief Advisory Committee, Mr Barry Greer, a Senior Public Servant who reports direct to the Minister.

This burned out building was the Prospect Hill School.

The remains of the Prospect Hill C.W.A. Hall.

# NURSES RAISE OVER $1,500 IN APPEAL

**Last Saturday nursing staff of the Strathalbyn Hospital pushed a bed containing a 'pateint' round the streets of the town to collect for the Bushfire Appeal. In the few hours they were able to spare they collected $1,530.54.**

Director of Nursing, Jill White, expressed her delight at the generosity of those who gave. The local residents, those passing through and visitors.

The money was collected in an assortment of medical necessities from bedpans to wash bowls!

"Bring out your purses to aid the Bushfire victims!"

## Meadows Appeal

As a result of numerous enquiries from people wishing to donate funds to assist those affected by the fire in our local area, the Meadows Council has obtained authority to set up THE MEADOWS BUSH FIRE RELIEF APPEAL to accept donations, to assist those who have suffered losses within this Council district.

Contributions can be paid direct to either the branch office in the Main Street of Meadows, or at the Civic Centre, The Hub, Aberfoyle Park and cheques should be made payable to THE MEADOWS BUSH FIRE RELIEF APPEAL. Donations of $2.00 or more will be tax deductible.

Funds will be administered by a Committee headed by the Mayor, Geoff Simpson, and including the Rev. Colin White and Mr. Harold Leach, both residents of Meadows who, although not directly affected by the fire themselves, have been very much involved in the provision and co-ordination of voluntary assistance to those who have lost property and stock in the fires.

**FIRE FIGHTING STILL OCCURING AT MEADOWS**

C.F.S. and volunteer fire fighters are still in the field at Meadows fighting fires.

These men are concerned that their employers will have the opinion from media releases that the fire fighting has finished and their jobs will be in jeopardy.

Recent T.V. coverage of bushfire areas in the north show people celebrating the end of the fire.

It is stressed that this is not the case in the Meadows area and it is hoped that employers of fire fighters at Meadows realise this.

Gwen Willsmore and Joan Parsons, both of Normanville, from Yankalilla Red Cross, working at Meadows distribution centre.

## A DAY OF TRAGEDY

The bushfire in it's fury swept
Lives were taken, homes were wrecked
Searching here, searching there
The wall of fire was everywhere

The high wind helped this vicious force
So many fought with sad remorse
Though hearts are broken, spirits low
We must go on as life will flow

And happiness again prevail
As we live on to tell our tale
Perhaps one day we'll understand
And take the [illegible] of our land.

by ANNE HALE

This street stall run by the Strathalbyn Senior Citizens last week was in aid of the 'Bush Fire Appeal'. Local Senior Citizens members helping are from left, Edna Borrett, Elsie Heinrich, Una Jarvis, Norm and [illegible] Robertson, Jean Lamshed and Alby Bonham. With money raised from the stall and donations collected the total is approximately $400.

PAGE 8 The Southern Argus, Thursday February 24th, 1983

Figure 22(b). Holocaust Wednesday continued, *Southern Argus*, Thursday, 24 February 1983, p. 8.

and looking to the north and seeing the huge pall of smoke. When I saw all that smoke, I simply had a great fear of what I was going to find, and whether, in fact, I was actually heading right into the fire. And coming up on that road from Upper Sturt, you couldn't see any flame or anything like that. It was just incredibly thick smoke – of course, it was burning all those houses up along the ridge up towards Mount Lofty. I got onto the freeway and was heading back towards Mount Barker and I was probably doing 140-plus kilometres an hour, and a police car came down onto me – came up behind me, gave me a couple of toots on the horn, where his passenger wound the window down and said, 'Be careful, driver. Good luck.' And then he sped off. At home, by the time I got there, the worst of it was over. The fire that was heading towards us on a huge frontage had been stopped by a farmer who had put out a line of sprinklers across his property and stopped that section of the fire that was coming through. Then my wife and I headed back to my wife's father's property, which was at Ashton, and found her father pretty distressed, although he'd stopped the fire from crossing the property, but at a great cost. He had a heart attack about three months later, and we believe it was due to the stresses of that fire.

The fire had a tremendous impact on Prospect Hill. Regrettably, there were two people that died in that fire, just down the road. Joyce Smart, our curator, had a very narrow escape. The museum, I feel very sad when I see what we've got at the museum, and then realise what was destroyed in that fire. It makes me very sad. But of course, there were some miracles: the fact the fire got into the museum itself but was able to be put out by a fire truck that went through the area. So let's hope we never see anything like that again. Perhaps we are a little bit better prepared for it as well. Following the Ash Wednesday bushfires, more efforts have been put into protecting and preserving the built heritage of Prospect Hill. There is now underground piping, there is a large pump in the shed up the top of the hill connected to various tanks. The museum itself has got sprinklers across the roof. And overall, it's much clearer – cleaner than what it was those thirty-odd years ago.

Prospect Hill's built heritage and heritage stories have helped residents to recover from the bushfires. I suppose, initially, it would have helped people to discuss the fire and how it affected them, and it would have been easier for them to maybe not dwell on their own problems, but thank the Lord, George – you know, 'I was pretty lucky. Poor old George lost all his stock'. So I think it's also important for newcomers to learn and go through the Ash Wednesday exhibit and see the devastation, because people who want a lifestyle change and they've got to come out to the country from the city, and then they don't really appreciate what, or how bad a fire can be. And they become complacent. I can recall just a few months before that fire, a fellow had built a timber house up from Yarrabee Street, on Greenhill Road, and he was asked, 'Aren't you afraid of fire?' And he said, 'No, this is special timber, and it won't burn.' Well that place simply exploded. It was sheer ignorance. So it is important that people, when they come into the area, they should come to our museum and they should see what the devastation was.

The Prospect Hill community today faces a big challenge. There are some very willing and able people here that do their utmost for the community, but we need younger people to come on and pick up the tools and help in the work that's necessary. The buildings here require maintenance constantly – it's the same as anyone's house. And if people are just sitting back and they say, 'Oh, well somebody else can do it' – that's not on. So I suppose the community, like many organisations, face the problem of lack of willing helpers. Of course, everyone's got their problems: they've got kids at school, they've got football. But you can't leave it all to a few people. And that's the big challenge – to get more people involved in this wonderful community and make it even better from their input as well as those people that have gone before them and put in their input. People say: why do you do that? Why do you go every weekend to Prospect Hill and sometimes the meetings in the evening, and sometimes if the Scouts want a late or an evening through the museum, we'll open it up. I think because I had such a wonderful childhood here, I'd like to put a little bit more of me back into the community. That's why I do it.

18 November 2014

# Jack Lovelock

Figure 23. Jack Lovelock, 15 November, 2020. Photo: Jiayuan Liang.

I have lived in the Prospect Hill area all my life, eighty-one and a half years. My father came here in 1927 and married my mother Mabel Connor. He previously lived at Bull Creek and purchased the farm here before he married my mother. I'm a dairy farmer. Have been since I was fifteen. We also grow potatoes, and we grew peas. When dad came here, the farm was all scrub, and it had to be cleared by hand in those days. With two horses, a disc plough, a grubber, and an axe, and a saw, and a wallaby jack. Most of the clearing was done that way. They would anticipate or try to clear about five acres a year. The timber was just pulled together and burnt. The ground was worked with a plough and most of the time, I think, a crop of potatoes was put in. But the soil being so sour after having trees on it all its life, crops weren't very much. In later years, when super[phosphate] came in – because there was no super in the days when Dad started – that and the Mount Barker clover was what really made the farming here in this area. The Mount Barker clover is a sub clover, and once you sow it there, it regenerates every year. In more recent times, there's a lot more variety of rye grass and clover now planted, but the Mount Barker still persists and that makes really good hay.

I run the farm with my son, Andrew, and grandsons and my wife, Christabel. The farm has grown from a hundred and fourteen acres to over four-hundred acres here that we own ourselves. And we also rent about four-hundred-odd acres in this area. There is about three-hundred dairy cattle. Then there's the heifers, and the other farm we got away from here, that runs beef cattle. That's down in Geranium; two-thousand acres there. Our dry heifers and that are reared up down there and then brought home here. We supply and sell the milk to Dairy Farmers.

Our house is located right next door to the Prospect Hill Church, a Methodist church. One time, when the people were all at the church, God was first in their life. I can remember as a child, in the morning services, there would be between fifty and sixty people attend. And the night service, there would be probably thirty. There would be about forty children on the platform of an anniversary. And it was the main thrust. Back then, we had a resident Minister in Meadows, and the circuit was comprised of Meadows, Ashburn, Bull Creek, and Underwood. And the other

Figure 24. Jack Lovelock standing beside ANZAC memorial outside Prospect Hill Wesleyan Methodist Church, which opened in September 1873. Photo: Jiayuan Liang.

circuit was Clarendon, Kangarilla, and down that way. But the circuit here, it changed and it brought in Clarendon, Kangarilla, Prospect Hill, Meadows. And Ashbourne went to Strath. But the original one back, years back, was from Clarendon. And the pastor used to ride horseback out here to take the services, as well as local preachers. Back when I was only a lad, the community revolved around the church. There was no other buildings to have entertainment or anything, and everything revolved around the church. That was my main interest, and always has been, really.

I was an avid tennis player, and also table tennis. That was my main thing in the community. I was also a scout for a while in this area. We had a full table tennis team, like an A and B-grade team, and that went on for quite a few years from about the forties onto the fifties, sixties. At first, years ago, it started off in the church. We used to have it in the vestry at the back, and when the community built a hall, it moved up to the hall. And that's where it grew, because we had more room. There was an association. Just after the war, the Second World War, the church needed a piano. We had a concert party. The young people would go around to various places like Strathalbyn and towns out around and we collected enough money from the concerts to buy a piano. And that was put in there in memory of the soldiers. And that's still in the church now.

But as things have changed, people just don't put any credence, really, much on that. They can do it all themselves and they don't rely on God for anything – that's the way I see it. And that's how the District has gone now. I mean, the congregation now is down to about fourteen, fifteen, sometimes we get twenty. At the moment, we haven't got a resident Minister because there's just not enough congregation to afford it. And the same with Meadows, they're on their own too. But we do have a pastor that comes once a month. The first Sunday in the month, we have Communion that day when he's there. But other than that, we have preachers from Adelaide and all around the Hills. The struggle there is to get the message out to people, and you don't find that easy. But there is one good thing about it: three young girls joined the church last week, in their twenties.

In terms of the history of Prospect Hill, I suppose the pioneers coming out on to scrubland and clearing it to make a living, I would consider that to be the most important aspect. I think they tried mining, but there wasn't much in it, and that ceased. Because it was very hard in those days, and the roads weren't very good, and communication wasn't very good. They had a flag on what they call Flag Tree Hill. They would know from that, with other flags on Mount Lofty and further around – when the flag went up, they'd know their boat had arrived in Port Adelaide.

Long before my father was here, the Griggs family had a very large orchard that was planted by George Griggs, the father of Mr W.J. Griggs. Mr W.J. Griggs was a man that really looked to the future of the district itself. He was a great church man and a local preacher; he was the organiser of getting the telephone, and he had the post office at Prospect Hill and the shop, and there was a petrol bowser there as well. My grandparents had a grocery store next to the church. So there were two shops in Prospect Hill at that particular time.

Mr George Thomas Griggs employed quite a few people. His father had some grapevines and they used to make wine. The cement pit where they made the wine is still there. In the latter years Mr William Griggs used it for a silage pit. My mother, Mabel Connor, told me that Will Griggs' grandfather was killed at the Blackwood railway crossing, either coming home from, or going to, Adelaide. He had been drinking. After that Will Griggs' father, George Griggs, pulled out all the vines and would not have anything more to do with drink.

My grandfather, Alexander Connor, owned the grocery store. He was the foreman in the Kuitpo Forest and his wife, Julia, ran the shop. In the early 1900s he planted the regeneration block, about a mile from the Forest Headquarters. It has a mix of pine trees and different varieties of gums. It is a thick forest. It is still there today.

His two sons, Alexander Hilton Connor and Royal Laurence Connor, worked at the forest for a time. After that they ran the bus service to Adelaide. They started at Prospect Hill, picked up passengers from Meadows and through Clarendon and Blackwood. The bus service consisted of two Buick passenger cars, each capable of carrying seven passengers. One left early for people working in Adelaide. The other left half an hour later. For the

Figure 25. Milking time, W.J. Griggs. Undated, courtesy Glenys and Graeme Usher.

journey home, one left Victoria Square at 4pm and one left at 5pm. There was a bus station at Grote Street at that time, where the cars were kept during the day. Several bus services from the countryside (Stirling, Woodside and other places) parked there, near the GPO. One car ran on Sunday nights, leaving around 4pm from Prospect Hill, for people who worked in Adelaide but stayed in Adelaide during the week. This was over about 10 years before the 1939–1945 war. Alexander (Heck) Connor sold the business to Bill Robinson before the war ended. After that, the service started from Meadows and we had to ride our bikes to pick the bus up at the corner.

Mr Griggs employed quite a few people; they had a sawmill there as well that they used to be able to saw out timber. With the two factories in Meadows, there was a lot of wood carting and quite a lot of people got their living through cutting wood. And it was cut into what they called a cord, which is a bit more than a ton. And it was cut into about four-foot lengths, loaded on the truck, and then it was taken for the boilers at the factories.

Figure 26. (a) (above) Dave Sheppard on horse and Jack Palmer standing

(b) (Right) Harry Palmer and brother with horses and dray.

(c) (Below) Children and friends of the Palmer family. Jack Palmer second from left, holding the horse. Blackfellows Creek, 13 January, 1929, photos courtesy Glenys and Graeme Usher.

And also there was one chap that used to cart a lot of wood to the brick kilns in Adelaide. And that was another income for the people in the area. There was a lot of wood cutting. When I was going to school at Prospect Hill, you'd see probably two, or three, or four trucks a day go past loaded with wood to either Adelaide or factories.

The Griggs family had sheep, as well as dairy cows and pigs, and the produce from that used to be taken to Adelaide with a van and four horses. Well, my grandfather – his father died young – and Mr Griggs took my grandfather on at ten years of age. My grandfather drove the van and the four-horse team to Adelaide with the produce in the van. When they got to Clarendon, there were spare horses there. They used to hook two more horses on the front to tow the van up the steep hill to get it up on to the top, because it was a bit too much for the four horses. It was pretty well a full day's trip to get to Adelaide. They'd start early in the morning, they'd get there, you know, in late afternoon. Well, then, they'd unload and then bring supplies back the next day. My grandfather said when he first went the first trip down, where he went into the market, one of the men came out and he said, 'Oh, you're Mr Griggs' man?' The man called the other chaps around and said, 'Oh, come and have a look at Mr Griggs' man: a ten-year-old boy!'

Will Griggs was also instigating in the forties for getting the power through here, because in those days, it was only kerosene lamps, and hurricane lanterns too, you know, when you went outside. My grandparents owned the grocery shop for thirty-five, forty years. When they died, it changed hands. Ross Harper from Clarendon bought it, and it ran as a greengrocer shop as well as grocers then. But it only ran for about four to five years, I would say, and then it closed. And the shop up there nearly, practically closed. It was only sweets and cool drinks towards the finish. Keith Griggs – that's the son of Will Griggs – he carried the tradition on, and he was a great man for the community. And he was in the church. He was organist for, I don't know, fifty, sixty years I suppose. I've taken that job on myself now.

In the old days, when somebody was in trouble, everybody would flock around and help them, but you don't see that anymore now. I mean, the amount of dairy farms that were around within, say, two miles of the centre of Prospect Hill would have been probably thirty-five or forty dairy farms. Now there's only two!

Our farm, when my family first started here, they only had two cows and they had to buy chaff to feed them because there wasn't enough feed to really give them, you know, enough feed to eat. And they milked the cows and they made their own butter, and they would rear a calf or so from that. The farm, when Dad was there, there wasn't enough income. He used to get six weeks' work on the Council, and that would be with a shovel cleaning out the water tables. That helped him along. But when they first started here, really their living was mainly to shoot foxes, rabbits, and possums. And the possum skins back then – the brush-tailed possums – were thirty shillings a pelt, which was a lot of money. Dad even cut his honeymoon short to come home to possum. He made enough in three weeks to buy two horses and a plough – out of the skin money. That's how tough it used to be. The Depression was on then, and there wasn't very much money around.

Then, as the land gradually got cleared, there was more pasture. The cow numbers increased and then they would rear more calves until, oh, about in 1940. From the forties on, there was enough clear land then to run thirty-five cows. That was the main income then: the milk. But that varied at times. In the early days, the milk was churned into cream, the cream was turned into butter, and the skim milk was fed to the calves. Dad also had a few pigs, and that went to feed them. The butter was prepared, churned and made, patted up into pound blocks – all this done by hand. In the summertime, when it was so hot, they used to put the butter in the wheelbarrow, take it down to a well further down the paddock – which was a long way down – hang it down in there overnight to keep it cool, bring it up in the morning, pat it up early and then it went on the service bus to Adelaide where a chap met them there. They used to take it down to Glenelg and it was sold there. That went on for, you know, quite a few years until factories started to operate. Prior to the factories, it was dipstick measurement. They'd have a can of milk, and he'd just put a dipstick in and measure it, and they were paid on volume. When the factories came into being, it was fat. Paid on butterfat. But that's changed now; it's butterfat and protein.

After I left school – I more or less had to leave school early to come home, because Dad had a heart problem and he couldn't work so much then. I just worked on a share until I met my wife, Christabel. When we got married, the home here was the original home. I knocked that down, because my mother and father had bought the house next door which was really my mother's home. She was born here in that house, which is on the northern side of the church, where the shop was located. Then we built a small house here on the southern side of the church. That's been extended twice in our lifetime, until what it is now. The name of our farm is Glenrobin. We named it. We've got a Holstein stud which runs under that name. I went next door to the neighbours for quite a few years and managed that place, because there wasn't enough money home on the farm with two families. And then I left up there, and came home here when Dad, you know, they were both getting a bit too old to do it all. Then I built the herd up here till we were milking about forty-five cows and that went on for a few years. Grew about four acres of potatoes, probably an acre or two of peas, and we used to employ about eight or nine people to pick those peas back in those days. If you got six or eight shillings a dozen pounds, that was good money. Sometimes it wouldn't be that much, sometimes it would go a bit higher, and that was really good. And that's how it's been. I just kept milking the cows all that time, growing those potatoes for about, I suppose, ten to fifteen years. When Andrew left school he was keen to go on with the farm. We bought another block at Macclesfield. Over the next four or five years we bought three blocks of neighbours' properties, till now; we're up to a three-hundred cow herd.

Let me tell you about the Ash Wednesday bushfires. We had all the irrigation watered up the day before here. In the morning, when the fire first started, I said to my wife, 'Don't leave the house, because you'll be safe.' Because that paddock was green. I went to the fire truck at Blackfellows Creek. We had a young lad working for us at the time. He was at the house if it really got bad.

I was down at Blackfellows Creek fighting the fire, and at the fire shed. There were others from the community who were involved in the Blackfellows Creek CFS: Graeme Usher, Dick Ramsdale, Mervin Smart. Oh, I really can't think of the names of a lot of the ones. We went further down the colony. It was pretty horrendous because you were right in the middle of it. There were people there, I said to them, 'Look, you'd better get out, because you'll get burnt here.' They wouldn't come, they stayed in their house. Luckily enough, they did survive.

We got back to the fire shed, and the fire was coming up both sides of the road. It was like a steamroller about three or four feet high. Just a ball of fire, racing up the paddock. There was very little feed on it, but it was burning – even burning the dirt, nearly. And then that went through and we followed up behind and we saved quite a few houses. Towards the end of the day when I came home, we went back towards Meadows down to Laurel Road. We went down there because the fire was coming up from the northern side. And as we got down there, I said to them, my mate, I said, 'We're going into a terrible place here.' I said, 'We better turn around and get out.' Anyway, we got down there and it was burning up through the neighbour's property towards us. A shower of rain came. That put the rest of the fire out, and made it a lot easier, because that was getting on towards 4 o'clock in the evening.

I came back home here. The police had come in and told Christabel to leave. She said, 'Well, my husband said, "Stay! " He said, "No, you'll have to leave".' Of course, he was a policeman from Adelaide. Didn't know much about the area. Because prior to that, the local police had come through and said, 'Yeah, you'll be safe there: stay there.' Anyway, they finished up going into Meadows. There were people on the Meadows oval. They had petrol in the back of their cars. I mean, it was reasonably safe up there. But it would have been better to have stayed home.

We were fortunate our house wasn't burnt down. All we lost was about a hundred yards of fencing. Of course, the power was off. We had no power to milk the cows. They just didn't get milked that night. And then we had to chase around and get an engine to work the milk machine for the morning's milking. Because there was no power for about, oh, a couple of days when we were without power. So that was a bit horrendous. But I believe that the Lord protected us. We pray to God every day that He will protect us and I believe that that happened. It didn't actually affect me afterwards. I didn't have any real repercussions from it, but a lot of people did. It did affect a lot of people, for sure.

There were several homes up in Prospect Hill that did burn down. Those that lost their homes, definitely, that's devastation for anybody to lose their house. And the community. There was a small community hall with a library in it up there that did burn. And that had a historical library in there from the school. And they lost that. That wasn't an historic building, actually, because it hadn't been there many years, but it did take a bit of the history away from the library and that. And the other historical house up there, the Griggs', did catch alight on one end. But the other unit from Blackfellows Creek, the boys got in there and put that out. Because when we came through, everything looked okay. The other building was even standing. It was all burnt around, so we thought, 'Well, we'd better come on and see what the houses are down there.' And we'd not long left there, and it burst into flame.

STATE OF DISASTER

STATE OF DISASTER

Agony of another Ash Wednesday

Figure 27. Agony of Another Ash Wednesday, *Advertiser*, Thursday, 17 February, 1983. pp. 16-17.

Since the Ash Wednesday bushfires, more efforts have been put in to protecting and preserving the built heritage of Prospect Hill. They put in a sprinkler system around the house up there, now. I mean, it wasn't even thought of back before. For the old ones, I think, the older people, Prospect Hill's built heritage and heritage stories helped those residents who were affected by the bushfire to recover. Probably to get up and get running again, you know. Strive to do their best. I know there was one family that lived in the hall up there till their house was rebuilt. They were very independent. But they did get a lot of help from people. They were independent, but I think probably the heritage of that probably helped them a lot.

Since then, Prospect Hill has changed a lot. We've got a lot of new people come in here; people – they wave to me on the road as they go by, but I don't know their names, you know? There's a lot of people I don't know. Whereas, years ago, I knew everybody. Majority of the people now, that are in Prospect Hill, are newcomers. I think they're looking to really revitalise the heritage, by what I've heard. I think they'll keep it going, and probably still delve into things of the past. That's just my feelings at the moment.

12 March 2014

# Brenda Nisbett

Figure 28. Brenda Nisbett, 15 October, 2014. Photo: Antoinette Hennessy.

My parents were Cyril and Doreen Moore. I lived in Prospect Hill for 19 years until I was married in 1957. Our farm was at Blackfellows Creek where Chamel Field's property is today. We were always told that Blackfellows Creek got its name from a Negro who apparently jumped ship and who came prospecting for gold. On our property at Blackfellows Creek there was a mine shaft – I remember that very well – and my dad used to take us up there and we could look at it, but we had to be very careful that we didn't fall down it. I suppose it is perhaps all covered in now, I don't know.

I attended the Prospect Hill School, from Grade 1 to Grade 7. Miss Galley was the teacher. I played tennis and basketball, which is now known as netball. I attended the Methodist Church, now the Uniting Church, as it is known at Prospect Hill. I used to sing in the church choir and my dad, Cyril Moore, was the choir conductor for a number of years. At that stage there was no community association, but of course there were other organisations. I mean, the school was still operating, so therefore there had been school committees, and the church was very active so there would be committees attached to that. And the tennis club and everything was all very active. And so there were various committees associated with those things.

The CWA (Country Women's Association) hall was located where the community hall is now. I used to attend the CWA handicraft days. They were just days that the CWA ladies met, say of an afternoon, and did various handicrafts, like making cushion covers, and cane baskets, and a lot of handicraft in that respect. The CWA business meeting was once a month. There would be my mother, Doreen (Dene) Moore, who was a very committed secretary to the association, and my auntie, Gwen Coad, who did very well with handicrafts. Other members included Mrs A. Oakley, Mrs Audrey Palmer (Glenys Usher's mother), Mrs Vi Connor, Mrs Rene Connor, Mrs Claude Connor, Mrs Hurtle Michelmore, Mrs Harper, Mrs Pike, Mrs Gardiner, Miss Laurel Milligan, Mrs Doris Griggs, Mrs Merle Griggs, Mrs Bernice Griggs, Mrs Francie Griggs, and Mrs Gwen Howard.

Three members came from Mount Magnificent. They were Miss Effie Stone, Mrs Shirley Lewis and Mrs Hazel Stone.

The CWA ladies used to do catering for weddings. They catered for Graham's and my wedding at the Meadows Hall, so they were a very active lot of ladies. People would make handicrafts for themselves or as gifts. There were group competitions around handicraft making. I don't think the Prospect Hill CWA exists today.

Figure 29. Brownie Scout group from Prospect Hill, on a visit to Victor Harbour, 1953. Back row: Marlene Moore, Heather Cluney. Front row: Bronwyn Howard, fourth from left, Anne-Marie Foggo on the end. Photo courtesy Glenys and Graeme Usher.

I worked as a telephonist and a postal clerk at the Prospect Hill post office for four and a half years. The postmaster was Mr Keith Griggs. Amy Stone, she also worked there. She lived at the post office house. She was a cousin of Keith's – we were all related. The post office used to open from 8 o'clock until 10 o'clock on weekdays so you know if I finished work at 5 o'clock someone else had to take over. So Keith would have cows to milk and Amy would take over.

Prospect Hill was a particularly Methodist community in those days. There were a few families that belonged to Church of England, a family or so that belonged to the Catholic Church, but really other than that, it was mainly attachments to the Methodist Church. I would think the fact that most people were Methodists, that helped to shape Prospect Hill. There were a number of families – a lot of them were related, of course – in the era they grew up in, the church was a very important part of their lives. It is different today. A lot of people attended the church in those days, most families, which included Sunday School anniversaries. We had service, two services on those occasions and then on special occasions we had night services, and so it was really quite a centre point of Prospect Hill. It was a very friendly – a very friendly – community in those days. Of course, we now live back at Goolwa North, so we are able to visit Prospect Hill on various occasions, which is very nice. But it was a very peaceful community.

It was settled amongst the lovely hills and the pine forest. When I lived there, the population was approximately 160 people. It was a dairy farming area, with the milk being taken to the Kondoparinga and the Farmers Union factories at Meadows. A few men worked at the sawmill at Kuitpo. But most people then in those days were farmers, were dairy farmers. It was just a great place to be in the years that I was there.

I can't really tell you very much about the Aboriginal history. I can remember my mother saying that several Aboriginal children attended school when she was at school. But I think they were mainly State children that come to live at somebody's home for a period of time. But I can't really enlighten you on that. What a shame my mother is not here to be able to tell you some of these things. She was very knowledgeable, a knowledgeable person.

In regards to local heritage stories about Prospect Hill, I have heard the story of Sarah McHarg but my thoughts would really be centred around the Griggs family. The Griggs families were all very involved with the Methodist Church at Prospect Hill. My mother, Doreen, was the daughter of George and Agnes May Griggs. Anne Russell Spencer married George Thomas Griggs on the 10th of May, in 1866. They started their married life on a property at Tea Tree Creek, near Prospect Hill. Their first four children were born there. In 1872 they bought an acre of land from William Luftman. They built a pug house which is now the Anne Russell Museum. There were eleven children in the family and my grandpa, George, was the seventh child. He built his own house which is just over the hill from the museum. And it still stands today on the property now owned by my cousin, Michael Griggs, which is his grandson.

The eleventh child was William and the father of Keith Griggs. William took over the post office work from his father, George Thomas, and William's son Keith carried on the work at the post office. He was an only child, so he didn't have any brothers or sisters, but no, just a good fellow. When I think of Prospect Hill I think of Keith Griggs. Keith was a special person. He was a scout master, a church organist, played tennis, table tennis, secretary of various organisations, and the RSL, of course he was involved with. And he was always busy at Busy Bees. He had the ability to see the best in people and to be available to help anyone in need. And of course he was also a music teacher. So a lot of the younger people were taught music by Keith. Keith Griggs was just a great person for Prospect Hill.

Figure 30. Old Post Office Prospect Hill, c. 1890, courtesy State Library of South Australia.

My mother and father always spoke very highly of him. Both my mum and dad were very musical so Keith's interest in music was very interesting to them. I suppose I really got to know him when I went to work. He was my former boss at the post office at Prospect Hill. The post office was in the Griggs family for three generations over a hundred years.

By the time the Ash Wednesday bushfires occurred I had moved away from Prospect Hill. Graham and I were living at Naracoorte at that time. We were very concerned when we heard that the fires were heading towards Prospect Hill. It was very concerning for the people of Prospect Hill. A lot of damage was done. Of course, there were other places in the area that the fires also devastated. It was a very worrying time. My mother was living at Strathalbyn, so there were a number of telephone calls to my mum to check how various families were situated. We were just really concerned for the people. Mum would tell us what various properties had been damaged.

THE SOUTHERN ARGUS

The Southern Argus, Thursday March 3rd, 1983

PRICE PER COPY 20c

## Local Community Plays Major Role in Rebuilding Families after Fire Disaster

[illegible] Families, neighbours and the [illegible]ommunity as a whole will play a [illegible]ajor role in helping bushfire [illegible]ictims in the Adelaide Hills area [illegible]ebuild their lives, disaster expert [illegible]rofessor Raphael said in Mt. [illegible]arker recently.

"Now the immediate disaster is over, it is [illegible]tably important for families, neighbours, [illegible]elfare agencies and others in the local com[illegible]unity to provide long term help and support [illegible] those hit by this tragedy," Professor [illegible]aphael said.

[illegible] certainty about the future is natural among everyone involved – both victims and helpers.

"However, I understand people in the Adelaide Hills area have a strong community spirit and this will help to see them through as they rebuild their lives and communities.

"We have found this spirit is strongest in the early weeks. After that there is often a period of anger and disillusionment. This is the time when resentments can build and community ties break down.

"It is important for people to get through this time and work towards the common goal of rebuilding the community.

"The key factor will be for families and individuals to appreciate that the helping agencies such as community welfare, the churches, Red Cross, Lions and others are part of the community.

"They too can offer the skills and counselling that is very important as people go through the range of feelings they have in coping with this disaster."

Professor Raphael is foundation professor of psychiatry at the University of Newcastle medical school and consultant to the Commonwealth and NSW Governments on emotional problems that can be caused by disasters.

[L. to R.] Rev. Eric March - Strathalbyn Uniting Church, Professor Beverley Raphael, Jill Anderson - Ashbourne, volunteer worker, Pastor Wally Schiller - Strathalbyn Lutheran Church

### AFTERMATH

[illegible] Ash Wednesday II has, like its predecessor, [illegible]ecome history to the majority although it [illegible]ill remain a very real memory. Out of it has [illegible]ome a highlight in the story of South [illegible]ustralia, but what went into it too often [illegible]ecomes clouded and forgotten.

## Rotary Auction 'Thundering' Success

The Strathalbyn Rotary Club Monster Auction held at the Trotting Track on 26th February was an outstanding success. Both sellers and buyers were happy with prices, in most cases. Very few items failed to reach their reserve and of those that did not, private sales were successfully negotiated in several cases.

Possibly the greatest bargain, and certainly an unexpected buy, was a lot of four 'thunderboxes' which went for 50 cents, knocked down to a gentleman who happened to put his hand up at the psychological moment!

There were several well grown healthy potplants among the sale items which drew fierce competition among buyers.

A sign of the times was very obvious when a pony offered for sale had to be passed in, the highest bid being lower than those being offered for 10 bales of hay.

The associated stalls run by the ladies were also very successful, with brisk selling throughout the day and all left overs auctioned at the end of the day.

The profit from the auction will go towards community projects within the town and district.

The experts Graham Garwood and Jack Stanton making a close inspection of an engine offered at the Rotary Auction, while another remarks on the hosing.

## Daylight Saving Ends

[illegible]'t forget to turn your clocks back 1 hour on [illegible]urday night.

Figure 31. Local Community Plays Major Role in Rebuilding Families After Fire Disaster, *Southern Argus*, Thursday 3 March 1983.

To me, the CWA hall was very sad. Because a lot of work, especially with the CWA ladies, went into building that hall. Then we used to have social evenings in the hall, kitchen evenings and things like that. That was our place of being able to meet because we didn't have a bigger hall, and so that was, that was sad I felt when the CWA hall was burnt. And then of course when the school was burnt as well. You think of all the years that you attended school and that. And of course I think Prospect Hill was very fortunate that more of the sheds – the buildings and that around the post office and the museum – weren't damaged more. Because a lot of memories were made in that area.

It is very pleasing to see the way Prospect Hill has recovered from the devastation of Ash Wednesday. Where the CWA was located they built a community hall. They have a very active community association at Prospect Hill now. I am sure that there would be other people who could add more to that, who were perhaps living in the area when it happened. It's good to see the way that they have continued to try to build it up again. And it's a good place. There are a lot of people who have come into the area in later years. They all seem to be working together very well to try and preserve the history which is at Prospect Hill.

By what I have gathered, following the fires, more efforts have been put into protecting and preserving the built heritage of Prospect Hill. Ash Wednesday made people more aware that a fire can do so much damage and take away so much history. I gather they are doing more in this way to preserve things if there is a fire, with more equipment that can be installed these days.

Today, things have changed. The Prospect Hill community association is being well organised by a very enthusiastic committee and all the residents of the area seem to give their support. That's the type of community that it is. Prospect Hill should and will continue to be a great place to live, I feel. Even though I moved away when I was nineteen, I still feel a part of that community. I think you do, although I lived at Naracoorte for 26 years. I have lived at Naracoorte longer than I have lived at Prospect Hill, but you still come back. Prospect Hill is where I grew up.

15 October 2014

# Glenys and Graeme Usher

Figure 32. Glenys and Graeme Usher, 17 November, 2014.
Photo: Antoinette Hennessy.

*Glenys:* We are Glenys and Graeme Usher. My maiden name was Palmer. I lived in the Prospect Hill area for fifty years, total. Ten years of my life, we moved down to Point Sturt when we married. The last seven years, we've lived here in McLaren Vale.

Figure 33. Prospect Hill school students, 1953, with teacher Mervin Wray. Photo courtesy Glenys and Graeme Usher.
Back row: Gilbert Haywood, Alex Kuchel, Leonard Burman, Ken Michelmore, Ivan Code, Trevor Griggs, Clarrie Pike, Coralie Pike, Jocelyn Griggs, Marlene Moore, Heather Clooney, Maxime Miller, Caroline Griggs, Alison Harvey.
Middle row: Robert Usher, Anne-Marie Foggo, Anne Griggs, Bronwyn Howard, Glenys Palmer (later Usher), Margaret Haywood, Mr Mervin Wray, Rhonda Brown, unidentified Miller, Rosalie Code, Brenda Harvey, Wendy Howard, Erica Connor, unidentified.
Front row: Kevin Griggs, Ronald Bailey, Graham Haywood, unidentified, Leonard Buttle, Peter Cursive?, Billy? Haywood, unidentified, John Usher, Garth Palmer, Peter Foggo.

*Graeme:* We lived thirty years in Blackfellows Creek Road. At Blackfellows Creek. It's just a small collection of houses that follows the Blackfellows Creek.

*Glenys:* Our property had a name: Poltarilla. I think that's what Uncle called it. The area really is farming properties just joined together. And follows down the Blackfellows Creek Road. I went to school at Prospect Hill. I grew up there, was born there. I went to Brownies, played tennis, netball, table tennis. I went to the Sunday school. Later, I became a Sunday school teacher, and I was a member of the Community Association. Done thirty years with the Country Fire Service (CFS).

*Graeme:* I was involved with the Community Association and the CFS, the tennis club, table tennis club. And, yeah, just generally involved with the community while we were there for thirty years.

*Glenys:* We're both Community Association Life Members and Blackfellows Creek CFS members. I was secretary/treasurer of the Community Association for many years. I worked around the museum. In my really early days, I was very involved with my parents in raising money to actually build the present memorial hall. We're both – Graeme and I – we're very heavily involved in building the new tennis courts: raising the money and doing the physical work up there – building the tennis courts. CFS was just part of our lifestyle. We worked in the station night and day when required. After Ash Wednesday, we formed a Total Ladies Group. We did our training. Mostly, it was radio room I did, and catering. With the Community Association, I did a lot of catering.

*Graeme:* I was chairman of the Community Association for a while, particularly through the rebuilding period. I was Captain of Blackfellows Creek Brigade and then went on to be Deputy Group Captain of the Strathalbyn group.

*Glenys:* The community in Prospect Hill was like a family. We were concerned for each other. It was our life – our social life. You'd pack a basket of goodies and you'd pool your food, and it was just a way of life. There was no boundaries. You went to help each other if there was a problem. Or just visiting – social visiting – and having a cuppa and get-together and helping each other out whichever way they could. It was like a big family. And you were caring – you cared for each other in those days. I grew up knowing no other way. I think it's been brought down through the generations. I do know from my mother and my father, both used to say that's how they grew up. You all lobbed in and helped each other. It's been born and raised in me, really and truly speaking. It's part of life. And your respect for people – you respected people.

*Graeme:* My background growing up in Bull Creek was sort of similar to Glenys. If you didn't work with the community, the community didn't survive. So that part sort of expanded as we got older and both moved back to Prospect Hill, it was just part of it. We just became part of the community and did what you could. And it's the only way small communities survive.

*Glenys:* I think Prospect Hill's history is really like a baggage of things. You had your own farms to run, whatever you did, whether it be the dairying or whatever. Sundays were always church days and we always joined in the congregation at church. It was just a complete package.

*Graeme:* It was always, I suppose, a core of families that were around, seemed to be forever. And then their families were there. But then there was all those people that were coming and going through the community that became part of the community while they were there. That sort of kept it moving and brought fresh interest into the place and kept things moving.

*Glenys:* I can't tell you much about the history of Prospect Hill before European settlement, such as the Aboriginal history of the area. Only what I read in the history books. Just the general stories.

*Graeme:* I've never heard or read of there being large communities there. There's not the obvious signs of it, not like when we're down at Point Sturt up on the sand ridges. There was the middens of mussel shells, metres deep where obviously they'd been there for a long time. But I would have thought it would have been more as they were wandering through from these areas through the hills to the sea, which was part of their trade routes in those days. And it would have been more – if they had any sense – summer hunting and keeping out of the place in winter when it was so cold.

*Glenys:* I can't tell you a lot about the early days of Prospect Hill, either, from European settlement. Only the stories my father used to tell me. There were a lot of woodcutters. My own father worked in cutting pines. Brought in extra money to supplement the dairy side of things of the farm. Real early days, it was just hard work milking by hand. My mother used to milk the cows for her parents by hand and keep household for her brothers. We led a simple type life. I think of Brenda Nisbett, who was Brenda Moore. They used to be our neighbours. And her father – we used to call him 'Spinker'. I remember the days of him going past along the Blackfellows Creek Road with them, all in the horse and buggy, taking them up to church, and to Meadows to do their shopping. Things like that. They're the sort of things that I can remember 'cause I was only born in 1947, so I don't go back that far. So that's the sort of things that I can remember. What about you, Graeme?

*Graeme:* Dad used to tell stories, going with his father from Meadows to Adelaide with the horse and cart. So I suppose that was very much of the pattern that they go take produce to market in Adelaide and come back whether it was a two-day trip, two or three-day trip, to do that. Luckily, we're a bit beyond that. As an even later comer to the district, I haven't got any recollection or even heard many stories of the very early days.

*Glenys:* In terms of historical figures important to the heritage of Prospect Hill there was, of course, the Griggs family. They were the centre of Prospect Hill, stemming from the Spencers there.

Figure 34. Grace Arthur standing by one of Alexander Connor's buses, c. 1940, courtesy of Jack Lovelock.

*Graeme:* It was always the Griggs. Tom? Keith's father.

*Glenys:* Will.

*Graeme:* Will. Will Griggs, and that was about as far back as I go. I did come into the area occasionally as a young teenager, and it was all around the centre of Prospect Hill which was the Griggs: Keith and his father. They were a big part of the community and the idea of helping out. Like during the Ash Wednesday bushfires.

*Glenys:* On Ash Wednesday, we were actually in the fire station. We were feeding and fighting the fires ourselves. I was part of the team feeding the firefighters and Graeme was part of the team fighting the fire.

*Graeme:* Yeah, we'd been involved for two days with the fire in the forest beforehand. We'd been fighting fires since Monday, which would have been 14 February. They were just smaller fires. A fire that started in the forest directly west of Blackfellows Creek

Station, and we knocked it – we were able to knock it down. Then it was just a matter of mopping up.

*Glenys:* We had spot fires from that one that were close to home.

*Graeme:* And then when we woke up on the morning of that Ash Wednesday, it was a shocker. It was already blowing again. It was hot. And we knew we were going to be in problems even to hold the area we were looking after.

*Glenys:* There's lots to tell about the experiences with the fire. There was a lot of confusion, frustration, it was frightening. You sort of had to pull yourself together and have a plan of what you're going to do. Because you didn't know what the fire was going to do. It was very confusing. All you worried about was keeping your own family and everybody safe. And that's all. We didn't want loss of lives, which did happen.

*Graeme:* When the fire started down at McLaren Flat, we knew we were in trouble. We spent all that day around the area pretty much inside the middle of that fire. We were pretty much the only brigade that was there all day because the others were all around the outskirts, out on the range, and then back around Ashbourne, Meadows. We were pretty much it until late in the day. Late, very late in the day.

*Glenys:* We thought the kids would be safer at the school. One of the girls that worked with us – Angie – took our kids to the primary. They had a pool at the school and such like. Angie was on her way back from Meadows when she got caught. So she headed up to the fire station, but the fire was coming at her. She ran down and jumped in Pat Connor's dam and pulled the tarp over her head. That's where she was. Well, when the fire had gone over, she came out of the dam. She jumped in her car and came over to the fire station. She had to drive her car through the paddocks – no fences left, in low little flames – and she came through and drove over to be with us. She just wanted to be with us. Wanted to be with people. She was wet through.

*Graeme:* The fire itself broke all existing fire behaviour knowledge that we knew at the time. We had never even imagined the intensity of it. It was only afterwards that you sort of put together: 'Well, yeah, that was understandable.' For instance, out on the road along the top down towards Mount Magnificent, there was small stones embedded in the bark of trees on the eastern side of the road. You realised that it was a firestorm, that as it went through, it created a vacuum that actually sucked those stones off the road and then embedded them into the saplings and trees on the other side of the road. Normally, fire behaviour is that it will roar up one side, and then when it goes down the other side, it slows down. But this fire was so intense that when it came over the hill onto the eastern side of the range, that area was already preheated, so it just exploded. The whole thing just went bang, because it was all scrub. And then the southerly wind just swept it right along the range to the back of Meadows. This was contrary to what we'd understood on all smaller fires. But because this was such an intense fire, it made its own conditions. Where we were on the farm, we were actually that close on the edge of it, it virtually just sucked the corner out of the hay shed. It came out of Kyeema and across the Oakley block of pines. That was a rolling crown fire. The amount of air it disturbed was just amazing.

*Glenys:* Anyway, while we were at the fire station, a gentleman from Strathalbyn came through – our cousin, Ross Stone. He'd rallied around the shops and got bread and filling for sandwiches to come and give us a feed so we had some food. While we were having a cuppa, we decided that we wanted to get our kids back with us. We didn't feel safe. We just wanted our kids for some reason. Ross came with Angie and I. We had another young lad from the fire truck with us. And Ross had thrown an axe in the boot of the car – well, the back of the wagon. We took off through the property down to the Blackfellows Creek Road. When we get down to the Blackfellows Creek Road, it's all covered in fallen trees. So out the fellows hop. Ross starts chopping up to remove this tree. The young lad, Michael, he grabbed the tree and burnt his hand. So we had to get him back to Meadows. But we got a clearance enough to get ourselves through to the forest break. We drove up the forest break and just drove to get our kids. We got ourselves out onto the bitumen road and got through, winding around these trees all down along the road. One section was still burning overhead when we drove through, heading towards the Michelmore property. At the police blockages in Meadows, we said we wanted to get to our kids and they were asking us if it was safe. But we said, 'Well we just come from there, so we just wanted to get our kids.' And that was just a driving force behind us to do this, so that's what we did.

We'd all get our kids home from school that day. We took them to Meadows. Meadows was in chaos. The whole of the oval was covered in cars, animals, horse floats. Whatever you could name. People with stuff just piled up high. And then getting to the school to get our kids, and they just looked at us. They were all asking us questions like, 'Do you know whether our houses are standing, Mrs Usher?' and this and that. And I couldn't, I just could not tell them whether their houses were standing. Kids were all panicking. They just wanted to know whether their families were safe. And you just could not tell them, because you didn't know what was going on other than your little patch. We found it was more devastating for the kids to be away from us. Better to go through it with us.

Figure 35. (Left) Violet Connor's house after the Ash Wednesday bushfire, courtesy Glenys and Graeme Usher.

(Right) Malcolm Oakley's house after the Ash Wednesday bushfire, courtesy Glenys and Graeme Usher.

*Graeme:* The impact of the fires on Prospect Hill – its historic buildings and structures – has been devastating. We lost a lot of history.

*Glenys:* One that really sticks out is when the Country Women's Association Hall went up in smoke. We had the Burman lending library in there. They had the library in the primary school but they moved that into the CWA Hall when the school closed.

*Graeme:* It was all books.

*Glenys:* They were original copies of all your old heritage books. They were back in the old original bound books that you just don't see today. And they were in there: those books. They all just went up in smoke. That was part of the history of the district.

That's been lost. You can't ever replace things like that. I think we've lost quite a bit.

*Graeme:* The fire had a big impact. It destroyed the facility of the tennis court. It destroyed several of the outbuildings, the scout hall, the old school. Prospect Hill probably copped more from the fire than any other little district involved. Because we were smack in the middle of it. And there was several houses, there was lives lost. It was a really big whack on a little community. It took a while for the news really to get out; that it had been. Other areas, like Ashbourne, copped damage on the eastern side. Meadows copped a little bit on the edge, and that was about it. Prospect Hill was probably the only town in the area, or village in the area, that was really impacted because it was right in the middle of the fire. Right down along that Blackfellows Creek Road, right down to Kuitpo Colony, there was a lot of damage.

*Glenys:* Without the CFS, it would have been a lot more damage.

*Graeme:* We did manage to save some. And then when the other brigades came through, they were able to put stuff out. But by that time, any damage was done. Some of the houses would have gone in minutes. They were just hit with balls of gas coming out of the pines. There was areas of the forest that were that intense that it took the top twenty or thirty feet out of some of the pines tree. That created gas balls that then went out ahead of the fire. Looked like one or two of them directly impacted on houses and it was just 'BANG'. Nothing anybody could do.

*Glenys:* Jenny and John Bogarts, the couple that were living there, were on their honeymoon at Kangaroo Island. Their friend, Jane, was looking after the place, with her friend, Warren. She came to me and said 'What do I do?' I said 'Fill up some buckets and be prepared'. That was on the Tuesday when there was a fire in the forest.

Figure 36. Remains of Blackfellows Creek Fire Station firetruck, burnt on site by Ash Wednesday bushfires, Prospect Hill Museum, 13 October, 2020. Photo: Jiayuan Liang.

*Graeme:* A neighbour went by on the Wednesday afternoon. He was just in time to see the roof go in, but he didn't know they were in there. We were worried about them and we just couldn't get back to check on them. There was no communication, no phone.

She had done everything right. The bath was full of water. The laundry tubs were full of water. It looked like they stayed inside the house. They were together on the floor with a dog. Maybe they got overcome by smoke. Thursday morning when I took John to the house we found their bodies. There were chooks and ducks and rabbits that were outside were all alive. The horses were all okay. We think they stayed in the house too long. We don't know why.

*Glenys:* The fire was too quick for the CFS to actually keep up with.

*Graeme:* I think we would have had more of a chance. But there was the CFS brigades in there that didn't know the area. We could have lost people in that – in the centre of that. You just had to get out of it. Let it go over the top and follow it behind. Which they did later on in the day and then the next few days. But the damage had been done. After things had gone through, there was brigades from all around started coming through the district to help mop up and clean up. That went on for the next fortnight.

*Glenys:* We was very involved over an extended period with it. Both fighting it and in the aftermath.

*Graeme:* I've never seen another day like it. There was nothing you could do about the fire. It went from the north to the south, like that. Bang. The trees were pre-heated. They just exploded. The leaves give off a gas and that just combusted. All you could do was try and keep people alive. The fire wasn't far from me, but I felt safe because I knew where I was. I knew where the gaps in the pines were. At one point the fire was close up behind us, and we were doing over 60 miles an hour on Blackfellows Creek Road, to keep ahead of it. Dirt road.

*Glenys:* We lost 95% of our fences. Afterwards, we had all the neighbours animals running around our property. Cats, horses, kangaroos, some cattle. We had to have a bit of a sort-out afterwards – send them back to their homes. Everything stopped. We had no power. We couldn't milk the cows.

*Graeme:* The rebuilding phase was very involved with lots of different things, depending on which building it was. There was a lot of work involved with cleaning up where we made use of local people with equipment – the tractors, that sort of thing – and a lot of hours given to cleaning up. And then when we started rebuilding, particularly where the Ash Wednesday exhibit is now, and that area. We had to find a lot of stone to get that building started. There was a lot of work with that, a contractor in to do that actual building work. The tennis courts, that was a big project. There was a group of people who were very keen on their tennis and the community. They saw the need to get that going again. We actually organised private funding to get it started. A lot of the work was contracted out. It was a big project to redo the courts and re-fence and set up the lighting, actually. It was a big project. We put down two complete new tennis courts, and repaired the other two. It was completely re-fenced. And the stone wall around there was all done. The other buildings, they were repaired and rebuilt as necessary with each building, depending on how bad it was. Of course, then, the community centre was completely rebuilt.

*Glenys:* We had funding organised.

*Graeme:* That was all funding from Wollongong Council.

*Glenys:* I think, following the Ash Wednesday bushfires, more efforts have been put into protecting and preserving the built heritage of Prospect Hill. I think it certainly has, in a word. They're more aware. Until you experience something like Ash Wednesday, you're not aware about the impact that some of the devastation these fires can have on you. And I think, certainly since Ash Wednesday, there's been a lot of effort going at Prospect Hill to try and preserve what we've got left.

*Graeme:* Part of my follow-up was to get somebody from CFS headquarters to come in and actually design a system so that we could make a decent fire-fighting effort if we did have something impact on the buildings, through a system of tanks and pipes.

*Glenys:* Sprinklers on the roofs.

*Graeme:* Sprinklers on roofs and that sort of thing. And there was a trailer pump put in the shed up there to pressurise lines. So that even if the truck hadn't got there, you could actually make a

Figure 37. Blackfellows Creek fire crew, c. 2010, courtesy Glenys and Graeme Usher.

*Back row:* Ann Morrison, Bill Gibson, Sue Bowman, Stephen Teakle, Jason Pattullo, Kym Simister, Derek Parsons, Lindsey Gibson.
*Front row:* Wayne Bowman, Stephen Hare, Ruth West, Graeme Usher, Glenys Usher, Jill Hawke, Stuart Rowley.
*Absent:* Barry Williams (President), Jamie Grundie, Dennis Gatehouse, Horst Lushington.

fire-fighting effort on one of the buildings with just a few lengths of canvas and the pump. You had twenty-thousand gallons of water to start with, but water was always a problem in the area. You had dams, but they were always a long way away. You would have had to push water a long way to go and everything, so we did set up that system. But it's thirty years ago now and people do forget a bit. So how conscious they are now of keeping the pumps started and keeping all that thing going on, I'm not real sure. But the infrastructure was certainly there to make a difference.

*Glenys:* Yeah, I think Prospect Hill's built heritage and heritage stories helped residents to recover from the bushfires. Our little bushfire display that's there in the museum: it's helping people. Because when we did that display – and I was part of that display – we all vented our feelings. We thought they were all buried and gone. But we vented them again. I think this is part of your healing process type of thing, you know. And I think it certainly has helped people. And it's there for other people to see.

*Graeme:* Because of the circumstances, we lost some very good people in that they had to move out. They couldn't recover. I think one group in particular. They started up a little market garden business and then it was destroyed. They had to just move on. We lost them. Pretty well straight afterwards, there was a night on the old courts. We cleared up all the lights. Just put on an open night for people to come in and have a night out with music and probably the only two-keg night Prospect Hill's ever had, I think. It was a good night, and that started it. Then, when we started rebuilding, it really give people time to put efforts in, and there was a big recovery: mentally, physically, and monetarily, I think, around the district. It did take time. And it was certainly a big effort, with a lot of people putting in a lot of time. But it did have a big healing effect.

*Glenys:* The Prospect Hill community is different to when I grew up there and when I lived there. It's probably because people are very, very busy with their own lives these days. In our days, the community was part of our lives. Today, you've got to make the extra effort to put into it. It's got to be part of your life if you want to do it. But it's just an extra thing for people to do these days. It was just part of our lives. In our days, we went to the post office. There were other things happening at the post office. Keith Griggs running a little store. If you wanted to do anything, like when I was in Brownies, it was held in the building which is now the Annie Russell home. It was all linked together in the days gone by. Whereas today, you've got to make the effort to go, and go up to the museum and be part of it.

I feel the influx of the young people who are taking on the interests and the caring for what's left of the history, for example, caring and maintaining the buildings and the restoring of the old engines, is wonderful. I think that's what Prospect Hill today is all about. That sort of thing. The struggles that I can see, it's always going to be the money side of things. It's always going to be a problem. To get the next generation to be interested in carrying on: this is going to be the biggest thing. Because we've got a lot of population that's coming and going these days, and they don't stay. At the moment, we've got some young ones there that are staying and having a go. And that's what it's all about, I think. They've just come through a month of where the museum's been open every day of the week, virtually. This sort of thing, in my days of working on the community centre, was unheard of. So I can see that it's coming along okay at the moment. And I'm quite pleased to think that it is.

*Graeme:* The big difference now than in the early days, it was agricultural based. And now there's very, very little. It's virtually become a dormitory.

*Glenys:* Because people are going out of the district to work, while we were working in the district.

*Graeme:* Like it's happened everywhere else: the outlying areas are just becoming dormitory villages and suburbs. And that brings a total change where you haven't got people with perhaps time available during the day like you used to have on the farms. You could put things off and go and do these jobs that had to be done around the community. Now it means weekends. Individuals just haven't quite got the time that they had. It's just part of the pace of life, and part of the change of life, unfortunately. It's not as good a life as it used to be. We still talk about the 'good ol' days.' Things have improved a lot in lots of ways. But people have become very time-poor, and small communities suffer because of that. That's going to be hard. It's the museum that's the heart of Prospect Hill now. It's gotten to the stage where it is bringing people through all the time to see it, because they're managed to keep it up – keep the heritage, and people are coming to see that. Which, when you travel yourself, that it is probably the biggest industry of the future is tourism.

*Glenys:* I just hope the gang that's in on the community centre at the moment can keep up their good work, because they seem to be going through leaps and bounds at the moment. For me, it's quite exciting to see it happening, because I'd been on that committee where we were trying to make it happen for years, and it just didn't happen. And I think they've come a long way.

*Graeme:* Yeah, it's quite exciting that it's children of some of the older families that are coming back into the district to keep it going. That's along with the other sort coming in. It does give Prospect Hill a chance to survive. We wish them well with that, because at the moment it seems to be going quite well.

17 November 2014

# Pat Connor

Figure 38. Pat Connor, 7 March, 2014. Photo: Antoinette Hennessy.

I am 96 and I have lived in the Prospect Hill area all my life. Might have been a little while away, perhaps. I lived a little while in Loxton, but it's been my home always. I was born at Echunga. My house was located at a place called Blackfellows Creek which was only about five kilometres from Prospect Hill and Prospect Hill's Post Office and Hall.

My occupation was at home because we are talking now about almost a hundred years ago, and people had to make a living how they could. I was brought up as a child getting money from catching rabbits, and my mother had a few cows. We lived mainly off the land. In Prospect Hill we had the old families that lived in a similar situation as we did ourselves. I suppose most of my life would have been what all others around the district would have done. People made their own living from their own work: milking cows, growing potatoes, keeping sheep. That would be the main things.

Figure 39. Mr Calico Smith's draper's van, Prospect Hill, c. 1880, courtesy State Library of South Australia.

For our pleasure we probably would go to a dance, a weekly dance or something, and occasionally to church. The things we would be doing is visiting neighbours and talking to each other, telling them what happened during the week and some of the things like that. But we were heading there to farm the land. It is good land, but it was covered with trees and other plants: rubbish, bracken fern and so on. So our parents did a lot of hard work clearing the land, only with hand tools really. They did a wonderful job and we all knew each other. We had all these families that had come there over the years for one reason or another, and it was a very happy community. I don't know how many people lived in the community. I have been asked that question many times. But I never fully knew where the community began and ended. Agriculture was a big industry. But there were other industries there. Pine forests, which were government owned, put a lot into the area. The pines grew up around there and they were milled close by, providing work for others. We got on very well with the Forestry Department.

Learning from my grandmother, she said that Aboriginals used to pass through there in quite large groups, travelling say from Adelaide, or where Adelaide is today, through to the River Murray. They used to follow where the birds and animals were to provide their food and they used to come through there, come to the houses and ask for food to help them on their way.

That pretty well sums it up, even from the 1840s onwards, the early days of European settlement. I think those that came there, they produced their own food mainly. There were certain things that had to be bought and they used to try and earn enough money to buy things like sugar and salt, perhaps, and things like that, otherwise they lived off their own properties. The longer they were there, the more they could produce and they could start selling. They used to sell food like butter and vegetables, particularly potatoes, back to Adelaide.

Prospect Hill has its favourite heritage stories. For example, some community members like to tell the story of Sarah McHarg. Sarah McHarg, that was quite an event that had taken place at

Figure 40. Elsie Bignell, who later married Tom Griggs. Grandmother to Glenys Usher (nee Palmer). Undated photo, courtesy Glenys and Graeme Usher.

that time. As it happened, in the very early days, there was a few survey lines to work out. They had different heritages along the row of hills above where I lived. That was called, it was an English name, at the time. It was called Out of Boundary Road, or something like that. Correction: Ridge. Now that was regarded as a survey at the time. But later on, when the official survey was done, it ran into this previous one and it didn't match up because the previous one started in Adelaide and it didn't match up with that one. So some alterations had to be made there, but it has all been straightened out. Sarah McHarg's father was a member of the survey team. He and another family living in McHarg's Creek – it is called McHarg's Creek these days – they used to be friendly together. Sarah McHarg had left Prospect Hill to go down and stay with the other family. And the very fact that they had no communication between them, Sarah got lost and then died at a place called, today, near Double Bridges. And that story lives on today.

Other stories are about the Griggs family. We had a wonderful postmaster, Keith Griggs, and his father there. The Griggs family were very important to Prospect Hill. They were a good living, honest, hardworking family. That is all the generations that I have known, about five generations that I can recall, and they were the real establishment of Prospect Hill. There are younger generations since that time – they were all good families – but I am talking about down to the one that we all love so very much. It was Keith Griggs in my time. Keith Griggs went to the Second World War and whilst he was away his wife died. When he came home, of course, it was great grief to him. Oh, he heard about it while he was overseas and it was great grief to Keith. But he was the sort of man who held his chin up and it didn't show.

Keith was the one who wanted to establish the museum as it is there today. Keith said to me one day: 'Pat, we are losing too many things out of the district, things like old implements and axes and things like this.' Would I be agreeable to help him establish this little museum? And I was very pleased to do so. Keith Griggs' house forms part of the museum today.

During the Ash Wednesday bushfires, the museum and buildings connected to the museum were hit. It had a dreadful effect because it burned most of it out, with the exception of the Griggs' house. The house was saved but all, all of the museum buildings and articles that were in it were all destroyed at that time. The fire commenced at around McLaren Flat and it travelled a way in a south westerly direction quite quickly and made a long line of burning material. The wind changed and brought the whole lot of it back over, Prospect Hill being one of the places, because it had such a wide front on it at this time. I had been a fire control officer for quite a lot of years, but I had just left it at that time. At the time I was living at Loxton. My daughter rang me and said that there was a fire out on Brookman Connor Road and so I said I would come straight down, which I did. I was on the fire unit not as an official, because I had left that, but on the unit for two or three days.

Figure 41. Prospect Hill Historical Museum at night, 13 October, 2020. Photo: Jiayuan Liang.

On one particular day I said, 'No, I am not going, I am scared of what might happen.' So I stayed home that day, and I feel that because of me being at home I was able to save my house. We had some water there and we had it fairly well cleared around the house. Luck was also another factor. When the fire came through, through the pines, through the Department of Forestry pines, it jumped over. My house was only about a hundred metres from the road. The road had a lot of rubbish on it and it burned that first, which slowed its speed down when it hit my house. We were able to use the water we had there, out of house tanks, to be able to quell that stuff and keep it away from the house, keep it from starting burning on the house.

It burnt out nearly all of the Forest Department pines and it is rather difficult to tell you what the distance would have been from McLaren Flat. I am not sure of where it stopped and changed directions. It was in the afternoon. I lost all my sheds, all my implements, all my fences, everything but my house. We were lucky in saving the house, which was good, because when you lose your house you've lost all photographs of the children and very, very important things. There was many, many people who lost their homes at Prospect Hill on Ash Wednesday.

Following the bushfires, a lot is being done now to preserve the built heritage of Prospect Hill. I gave some land at Blackfellows Creek for a new building to be put there to keep a fire unit in. Since that time the government has taken over. There is everything there now that open and shuts, that big fire truck and everything that you would ever wish to be in a place. It is very gratifying to see.

I can't really recall anybody saying that the bushfire really destroyed their life. Some were fairly well insured. And then there were other organisations that provided money for them to restore their houses. So, in the long run, it was a very unhappy event. But I don't think it made a lot of difference to the place, other than it has improved, by way of the fact of the government becoming so aware of the danger, that they put a lot more money into it. Most people are more aware of the fact of what can happen. Many years ago they used to get bushfires. But sometimes today we get, for some reason or another, some people have deliberately lit fires.

I can't comment on why they would ever think of doing such things, but they have done it. But they have been mostly controlled.

In Prospect Hill now, very few of the old families, or descendants of the old families, are left there today. Because there was a time when people left Adelaide or its surrounds and came out there and bought small properties. I can only guess that many of the people who came to Prospect Hill settled on small blocks and largely had to drive back to Adelaide to get work. Many of them sold out again at higher prices. They are only strangers to the few of the old residents who are around there. But that is not saying anything against these new people who are there. But they, of course, don't fully understand what has gone on before. Since that time there's been big changes and the community that is there at the moment doesn't understand what a pioneer's museum really means. It can easily slip away and not be a pioneer's museum, which can be happening at the moment. Apart from that, Prospect Hill is good land. It will produce many things, particularly in the vegetables; it grows good apples and plums and many other things and it will go on and it will progress even further. That's my idea of it.

7 March 2014

# Joyce Smart

Figure 42. Joyce Smart being interviewed by Jordan Ralph, 12 March, 2014. Photo: Antoinette Hennessy.

I live at Prospect Hill, along Milligan Road, beside the Kuitpo Forest. I'm eighty-three and I've lived here for seventy-seven years. I wouldn't want to live anywhere else. I think it's the most wonderful place in the world.

I'm a farmer. I was milking cows to start. I had a herd of cattle – milking cows. But then I had to go to beef cattle, because all us smaller farmers were disposed of as dairies. If you wasn't in a big way, the factories just didn't want you. They wouldn't pick the milk up. We used to have to sell cream to start with. You had to separate the milk and sell cream. But then they started picking up milk many years ago.

Figure 43. Prospect Hill Dairy Museum. 13 October, 2020.
Photo: Jiayuan Liang.

When I had my dairy, there were forty-two dairies here just in Prospect Hill. A lot of the people with smaller properties, they had a few cows, and they grew their own vegetables and that's the only way they could get to live. They'd have a few cows and sell some milk. But now, there's only two dairies left in the district, which is very tragic, really. I had to go to beef cattle when we were disposed of as dairies. And so it's just beef cattle that I have. I've got beef cattle now. At present, I've got about thirty breeders.

Then, when they got calves, you got sixty, you see? It's a very busy job. You've got to keep a watch on 'em all the time, that's for sure. I run the farm by myself. But I've got to have someone come and help me feed stock and that. I can't handle the big five-by-four rolls of hay by myself anymore. I could up till two or three years ago, but I have to get somebody in to help me like that, yes. But it's a wonderful life, anyway.

We've got two halls here where people can come and use them, and tennis courts. I didn't play a lot of sport. I was always too busy trying to work and run my own property. So, I didn't play tennis or anything, but I used to play table tennis. Oh, yes. We used to go 'round all the places, and they'd come here to play. We used to have an A and a B team, and it was quite good. They don't have that now. All the lads and that, they go to Meadows for football. They haven't got a football club or anything here, because we haven't got an oval for them to play on.

We have the church down there – the Uniting Church – and that's about all. We're only a little place, but we have a lot in it! I was involved in the church, earlier in my piece. I belonged to the Ladies' Guild and that for many, many years. But that closed down quite a long time ago. There's not many that attend the churches nowadays, I'm afraid. But we've got the Scouts. We've got a wonderful committee that runs that. I belong to every committee that's ever been around! I belong to the Prospect Hill Community Association Committee since we started that, which was back in the 1950s. And I've also been the secretary of Meadows Valley Camera Club. Meadows Valley Camera Club has been going for about fifty-somewhat years. I'm just starting on my forty-sixth year as secretary-treasurer of that. We're only a small club, but we're a very friendly club if people want to come. We always invite people if they want to come along and learn things

Figure 44. Prospect Hill Historical Museum.

(Top) Historical museum displays.

(Above and right) Scout Museum, Prospect Hill. October, 2020. Photos: Jiayuan Liang

about photography. We have prints that every month we show. We have judges that come there and tell you what you should do and what you shouldn't have done. So, we've got that where people can come and learn a lot. It doesn't take anymore to make a good picture than a bad one, I always tell them. So if they can come and get some information that'll help them. Photography's been a big part of my life, that's for sure. So that keeps me busy.

I also look after the Prospect Hill Historical Museum. I have it open every Sunday afternoon and through weekdays by appointment, with busloads of wonderful old elderly people. They are the ones that enjoy it when they come. Or children. We had seventy children the other day here all at once. That was a lively time! It was lovely. I started here at the Museum when Keith Griggs wanted volunteers. So Pat Connor and myself was his first two volunteers in 1968. That's how long I've been here! So I should know a little bit about the history.

In terms of the most important aspects of Prospect Hill's history, I've got to go back to the Griggs family. They were very Christian people. Mr G.T., or George Griggs, the first Mr Griggs, he married Anne Russell-Spencer from Clarendon. Then he bought this acre of land here and built this cottage and all the outbuildings. But he also started off the general store. So this is back in 1872. They had a general store. And he started the post office, and the mail. The mail would be brought here from Meadows by Mr Harry Rogers. He used to ride a penny-farthing bike and he'd deliver mail six days a week. So they had their mail delivered six days a week, and a general store back in 1872. And then his son William, he took over in 1914 when he married Laura Marshall from McHargs Creek. They built the other house which adjoins this and they shifted the store and the post office and that up there then, 'cause the first Mr Griggs – his health was failing.

Then when Keith come back from the Second World War, he took over because his father's health was very bad. So from 1872 till 1996, those three men ran that. I always think that they were the ones that started the hub at Prospect Hill. And it still is. This centre here is really the hub of Prospect Hill. So without them, Prospect Hill might not be here.

Prospect Hill was called McHargs Hill to start with. See, McHarg come here, but he was only a squatter. He didn't own land. So when Burr come here doing the surveys, pioneer families were taking up land. Mr McHarg, he had to shift on. That's why he went down the bottom of Bull Creek. He started squatting there, then he went on further. As people take up the land, he had to shift on. But he's still got McHargs Creek named after him!

The church is the way Prospect Hill got called 'Prospect Hill'. They didn't want to call it McHargs because McHarg had already gone anyway. This goes back to Mr G.T. Griggs too. They built their church in 1873. They were down at the church one day and Griggs arrived there with a new spring cart, and his horses and that, 'cause that was the only they could travel. One lady said, 'Oh, the prospects are looking up, aren't they?' And somebody said, 'That's what we'll call it! Prospect Hill.' So that is how Prospect Hill really got its name. A lot of people think it's to do with the prospecting with the gold mines and that down the Blackfellows Creek there. But it was really what this lady said: 'Oh, the prospects are looking up, aren't they?' So we can put that back to Mr Griggs as well, that he was the one that got the name changed. So from 1873, it was Prospect Hill.

There was a little bit of mining in Prospect Hill when they started off. They didn't find a lot. It was mainly alluvial gold. And then they had the big dam. There was a fellow on his moonshine that night when the flood come down. He didn't open the gates to let the water out. Of course, they lost all their equipment and everything. I think it was people from England that was running that. They couldn't afford to start it all again. There's still gold down there, they reckon. Course, it's private. It's been sold as private property. But there'd always be all these people going down there looking, hoping they would find something. They struck water in one of the mines, just when they were getting to a seam of gold. They never went on. They had to board that up because the water was still running. That was back in 1930, I think that was. And the water's still beautiful, clear water still running out of that mine.

But the miners used to come up here. They relied on the general store up here for their provisions and that. Mr Griggs was supplying food and all to them. The Griggs' baked their own bread here. They used to breed pigs. The only way you could keep meat in them days was either in brine or by smoking. So they had a big smoke room where they used to smoke all their bacon and their ham. They used to put all the smoked stuff in calico bags and hang them on the hooks up there on the roof. Mr Griggs' daughters used to make the bags. When you come in, you could get a leg of ham, or bacon and that in these white calico bags – that's the way they used to sell it. So it was very handy for them down there to come here for their food. So there was a little bit of mining. And there was obviously dairy farming. There used to be a few sheep and things like that kept. And then people later on started growing some potatoes, things like that. But back in them days, they was only dry grown, not like they do now with irrigation and everything. All the ploughing had to be done with horses, and everything had to be done by hand. So they definitely never got the crops and that like they do nowadays.

As for the history of Prospect Hill before European settlement – the Aboriginal history – I know they used to travel through here. Back up just behind my place, where I live, they used to walk through when the weather was changing. If it was coming winter, they say they used to live down around the lakes and that. Especially down around Goolwa, at Goolwa beach. They could live where all the cockles and that are. Then they used to shift down to the plains, down around like Holdfast Bay, which is Glenelg, and down in those areas. They used to carry all these cockles. I can remember as a child finding all these cockle shells, 'cause I always thought, 'Oh, gee, the ocean used to be up there!' But it's where the Aborigines used to walk through, and they'd stop and have feeds of these cockles, and that. But they did, they used to live around here. But most of the time of year, it was really too cold for them. So that's where they used to go, down on the plains and that, mainly. The name of the Aboriginal group that used to live around this area ... I know it starts with a 'P'. The Peramangk! That's them. They're the ones that lived around here.

In the early days of Prospect Hill, from early settlement, everybody travelled in horse and carts. A lot of the families, some of the relations, used to marry into each other. Like a brother and sister might marry a brother and sister in another family. And some of the properties, if somebody had a larger property, say if the son was getting married, well the father and mother would cut a bit of land off up in the corner of the paddock somewhere and he'd build a house up there. And then if they had another son, well they might cut and build another. So you'd get perhaps three members in the families living on one property in those days. That's why it was such a friendly family. Because father and mother and that was just down the road, or up the road. There was no doctors or nurses around. I always thought, to the young women, when they were having their children, how comforting it must have been for them to know their Mum and Dad lives down the paddock, or Mum and mother-in-law and that lives up the road. When they married into families like that, I always think how comforting it was for those girls. There was somewhere where they could go for help if they needed it.

There's quite a few of the families were married, like brothers and sisters and that. If there was problems anywhere, there was always somebody there to help each other, because everybody knew each other. It didn't matter what it was and they seemed to get on so well together, all of them. I've never heard any stories where they didn't. So friendly. Our community spirit went right back to the very, very early days. Because, like I said, if they didn't ride a horse, they had to walk. So they never went very far. They used to have get-togethers. Sunday evening after church, they'd have gatherings in their families – in their homes, and sing. Mr Griggs here used to play the concertina. He used to supply the music when they'd have evenings here. And Keith was a wonderful pianist and organist. So they used to provide a lot of the music and that when they had these get-togethers. Everything used to be just so friendly.

There have been some sad stories in Prospect Hill. I suppose the tragic one was about Sarah McHarg. When the McHargs shifted away from here, that's when Thomas Burr come here doing the surveying. He would be away most of the time. His wife, Mrs Burr, was frightened of the Aborigines, you see. So Sarah would come from down at McHargs Creek and stay with her. And that's how Sarah got lost, when she left that morning to go back home. There was no communication between the families. I think it was about a fortnight later. The Burrs thought she was home at McHargs Creek and the McHargs thought she was still up here, and of course she wasn't. So she'd been missing for nearly two weeks before they realised. And it was August, which was one of our coldest months of the year, when they started searching for her. It was two years before they found her remains down at the Black Swamp, down at Currency Creek. So that was sad. That was 170 years ago, last year, when they found her remains. When we had the plaque put up there in memory of her. I can remember, going to school, I'd walk past where she left that morning. And I'd always think on a cold, frosty morning – I could just imagine her going down through all that wild country. There was a track; how she missed that track ... My idea, because I always loved the fog and that, I love the foggy weather – and I always thought, I bet it was the thick fog that morning and she couldn't find the track. Because she would have known from here to McHargs Creek. She should have known that track very well. But she missed it somehow. That was one of the stories.

There were many old characters that used to live around here. There was this old gentleman, Mr Luftman, that sold Mr Griggs the first acre of land here. Apparently, Mr Luftman was a cat lover. He had this very large black tom cat that used to sit on his shoulder when he was eating. Mr Luftman was a great meat eater. But he never used a knife when he went to cut up his meat, he used a pair of scissors. So he held the meat with a fork and he used to cut it up but with scissors. Well, this one day – whether his tom cat was extra hungry, or the meat smelled a lot better than usual – the cat made one grab to grab the meat from Mr Luftman when he went to cut a piece off to swallow it. But the cat made a mistake: his paw missed the meat and he put his claw right through Mr Luftman's lip. They reckon the air was quite blue with bad language for quite a while afterwards! I never, ever heard whether the cat ever done it again or not, but I doubt whether he did. But that was one of the old characters that used to live around here.

There were some real old characters. They were all very harmless. Most of them wore beards, too, so it was a bit hard to tell them apart. I know. I had some uncles that used to live around here, and they all looked alike, because they all had beards! You couldn't hardly tell one from the other. Some of my great uncles, they used to walk. One, he used to walk from here down to the witchetty grubs. What the fishermen used to use. He used to grub them out of the rotting wood, and he'd take them down to Wellington to sell 'em to the fishermen. He had walked from Prospect Hill to there. He'd leave early in the morning, about 4 o'clock. He had seven children. His wife had passed away when she was thirty-six. She had just had twins. They both died. And then she died three days later. He was left with seven children to bring up. So he had to find some way of raising a bit of money for food. He'd leave at 4 o'clock of a morning, and those kids would be there waiting for him at night. He would have walked to Wellington, sold his grubs to the fishermen and come back again by dark that night. So I've come from a family of pretty good walkers! I'm not doing too good now, though.

Some of them, they used to walk to Adelaide. To the markets, to take food and that. The women would make their butter and that, and they'd walk to Adelaide. Yes, and if they had a young baby, they'd have to carry that on their hip to feed it on the way. You can't imagine what it was like. But that's the way they used to live. What they used to do. If you had a cow, and you had butter and cream and somebody else had some fowls, you'd swap. You'd give them eggs, and they'd give you butter and things like that. That's the way they used to exist.

There's some lovely stories and characters, historical figures, people who improved Prospect Hill. It was Mr Norman Brookman, from down at Brookman Road – he was the first one that found out about molybdenum for using it on the properties. It was really by a mistake that he found this out. Because the land was only all native stuff, there was no decent pastures or anything around. But when clearing properties out, they'd burn all the wood and rubbish up, and where the ash was, the feed, all of a sudden the grass and that just started to grow where they'd burnt and where the ash was. They found it was because of the molybdenum. When they started using that on the properties, oh, it just improved it so much. Mr Brookman also had a big apple orchard down there on Brookman Road. He supplied work to so many people, and the young people. A lot of the families would not have existed without having work. He was also the first one, I think, to export apples overseas. So that was really something for the district.

Another one I must mention is Miss Adelaide Mary Galley. She was our school teacher. She lived up here at the school that got burnt down on Ash Wednesday. It was on the reserve over there. She lived there in a little caravan. That reserve, in them days, it was just filled with all the wildflowers. She was a nature lover, so! I was just so fortunate to be going to school when she was teaching. She taught us all the names of all the native plants. She was a wonderful teacher. She was here for years. She used to ride a pushbike. She'd ride up to the junction up there … from Willunga, Kalangaroo, and Meadows up there at the 'Fingerboard', as we called it. And she'd leave her bike there and get a ride to Adelaide on a Friday afternoon. There'd be a bus go down. She'd look after her elderly mother down there and then come back on Monday ready for school. Her old pushbike would still be there waiting for her when she come back. Nobody'd ever touch it. She was a wonderful person. She taught forty-two children in one classroom. Seven grades. She taught us all herself. Of course, we did respect her, too. You'd never answer Miss Galley back. And she respected us. I'm sure she made such a difference to the lives of so many young people from around here. She was a wonderful person.

There's been so many lovely people around here. Prospect Hill has always been a community other communities have envied. The community spirit in Prospect Hill, it's always been wonderful. We owe a lot of our community spirit to Keith Griggs. He was known as Mr Prospect Hill. And rightfully so, too. He was a wonderful man. Keith was always there to help anybody. Didn't matter who it was. I always thought Keith was the one that made Prospect Hill what it really was.

Figure 45. Prospect Hill Public School reunion, courtesy Glenys and Graeme Usher.

Things have changed so much in the later years. A lot of the bigger properties were cut into smaller ones, what we call hobby farmers. People come out here and buy a small block. But they can't make a living off of a small block. So they have to go to the city to find work, or further afield. There's so many of them; the driving that they have to do every day – the mileage. They leave in the morning in the dark, and they come home in the dark, and you don't see much of them. That's the problem. It certainly changed a lot. 'Cause many years ago, we were all sort of one big family! You knew everybody. Especially when it was mail time. Everybody'd come up to the post office here to pick up their mail at the same time, so they'd see each other! It's just changed so much nowadays. Some stay for years. Some of them, they don't stay for long. After some of our beautiful wet winters! And summertime – the thought of fires and that – that frightens a lot of them away.

Like the Ash Wednesday bushfires. They were terrible. February the sixteenth, 1983. Oh, it was a shocking day. The temperature was a hundred degrees and the wind was about a hundred kilometres an hour. When I first knew the fire was coming, I was down at the fire shed – Blackfellows Creek fire shed. I'd been helping there all day. I saw another lot of smoke, and I made for home, quick as I could. I had some of my cattle down the bottom of my paddock. The dry cows, and a new bull I'd bought about three days before – he'd cleared out, hiding; he wasn't very person friendly! Anyway, I went down the paddock and I started trying to bring them up because there was so much grass and scrub, and the Kuitpo forest with pine trees over a hundred feet high right against my property. My milkers were up the top – the ones I was milking. So I brought that lot of the dry cows up through, and I just got them up there, and that's when it started. 'Cause when you put cows together after they'd been apart for a while, they all decide, 'Oh, we'll all fight each other to see who's boss.' So that's what started.

And then the fire went through McLaren Flat. It went right

through and across down through Mount Magnificent and it went right down to Double Bridges at Currency Creek. And the wind changed. It changed to a Southerly. A Southerly come in, which the old people – they'd never, ever known a fire coming from the south. They'd always said, 'Oh, you never got to be frightened of getting burnt out when it's from the south. It's never, ever happened.' But I'm afraid this time, it did. It come with the same force as it did from the north. It come right back up through from Double Bridges, right up through McHargs Creek, and right back up here. And that's when it took Prospect Hill out here. I'll never forget that.

My cows had all run into a corner of a paddock, up a bit of a hill by a dam over there. There was no way they'd get out. There was high grass and blackberries. There was a lot of blackberries around the dam and they all burnt. So I rushed over there. I had my little dog in the car and I was looking after a sick dog of my Auntie's. I put them in the car, and me pet possum was in the car! The little dogs were terrified when the fire come all around. When I could see the fire coming, I'd grabbed a big old bedspread and I put it in the car. I went over there. The flames was going across this bare paddock that I had there, which I thought nothing had ever burnt. There was nothing there to burn. But the grass was on fire. The flames was about eight foot high, just going across this paddock. I got across there in my vehicle – my car with my dogs and the possum in it.

These cows, I called them, and they started running down this hill where the flames were – running through the flames to me. I'll never forget the sight: they were holding their heads right up in the air, keeping their eyes and their mouths – trying to – [keep] out of the flames. And of course their tails. They got their hair burnt off their tails. They were milking cows, so you can imagine what their teats and that were. Oh, but then they milled around me. They stayed all around this one little spot. I was just in the one little spot that didn't burn.

There was two little calves let out, that was up in the yard. Two little ones I was feeding by hand. I saw them just going when this great big patch of scrub went up in flames. And I thought, 'Oh, that's the finish of those.' A while later – 'cause I lost all track of time – you wouldn't know how long it'd been. It just went pitch black when the fire was all around. You couldn't see, you couldn't breathe. It was terrible. And I felt something hit me in the back of the legs. And I put my hand down, and there – these two little calves. They'd come down 'round the edge of the fire, and they'd found me. Way down by the part of the property where I was with the cows. And they found me. They were sort of snuggled in against my legs like I was an old cow. And they stuck there by me. Some of the cows would go to walk away, and I'd call their name – because they all had names – and they'd all rush back. They all hung around, the whole forty-two of them. And there was this great big old six-foot kangaroo there amongst us. He thought, 'Oh, gee, I reckon I'm a bit safer with them.' So he was in amongst us. And this bull that I'd bought, that I hadn't see for two days, he was arrived there, too. From then on, we got on very well together. He thought, 'Gee, she's not too bad after all. I think I'll hang around here!'

I got down in the dam – course the dam was nearly empty – and I got there, and I got bogged in this mud when the fire was coming. That was a terrifying thing! But I managed to get out of it and grabbed this old bedspread, made it wet and threw it over the windscreen of the car, so it wouldn't get too hot. 'Cause I thought it might explode, you know, with the dogs in there. But, no, I saved all my animals, thank goodness. Out of the forty-two, I never lost any of my animals. One had its lungs full of smoke. For weeks it coughed and coughed. But no, I never lost one of them. Was weeks and weeks and weeks treating them with cream, bringing them in every day. I had to dry the cows off. Most of them, you couldn't keep milking. Their teats were too sore. Of course, they were blaming me for it when it hurt that much when you went to milk them. I'll never, ever forget that day. I said, somebody was with me that day. That's for sure. I was very lucky. On seventy-two acres, I was in the one little spot that didn't burn.

When I drove back across the paddock, took me car and the dogs back, everything was on fire, of course. I got there. All the hoses was burnt, everything. I thought my house was still there. But it was all on fire inside. I went inside and grabbed a couple of things. I'd won this special nature trophy at Camera Club on the Saturday night, and I thought, 'Oh, I've only got that for twelve months.' I had it in the special place where I knew I could grab it if I needed to. I don't know why, but I had. And I grabbed this trophy. It's still being used here at Camera Club now. Thirty-one years later, the same trophy. I saved that. But, oh, it was dreadful. When you see your house just explode and you can't do a thing about it. I had my face and all burnt. I didn't even know that till I had to go up to the Meadows.

The kangaroo stayed there. There wasn't a blade of grass for cows; you had to have the feed brought in. The kangaroo would be there every morning, ready for some hay and that with the cows. He stayed there for about three weeks. One morning he'd disappeared. I thought, 'I wonder where he's gone?' He was gone for three days. He'd gone and he'd come back; he'd found a mate – a female. He didn't bring a male, he brought a female. But out in the forest, six weeks later, the rangers were finding the kangaroos. They were still alive with their feet burnt off. They had to go destroying them. But now I've got over a hundred kangaroos on my property. And when they knock my electric fences and that down, or smash my fences, I say to them, 'Look, if I hadn't have saved your great-great-great grandfather on Ash Wednesday, I wouldn't have all of you! I wouldn't have all of you here now!' They know they come onto my property, because they get shot on others. So I'm feeding about a hundred kangaroos as well as my cows.

So, that was Ash Wednesday. Some of the people, they just couldn't cope with it afterwards. I did. I built my home again, on the same place. I'd been all my life buying my property and then when everything got burnt on it, I thought, 'Well, I'm not leaving now.' People'd say to me, 'Get out, get out, why don't you!' I said, 'No! I spent all my life buying it. I'm not going now!' So I'm still there. Some people, it took a real toll on them. Some of my relations that lived there, it wasn't long and they passed away. They just couldn't cope with it. We was very lucky that this museum building wasn't burnt. All the outbuildings were burnt. They had to be rebuilt.

If I hadn't done the right thing that day, well, I wouldn't be here, that's for sure. The day after Ash Wednesday, that was on the Thursday, I had about four great big detectives come there, telling me off because I didn't leave. When the fire was roaring down close to my property, I heard somebody yell. They told me that I had to leave. But I didn't leave. I went over the paddock with my cows. Course nobody knew where I was, or anything. But I would have lost all my livestock and they were my livelihood. I needed them and they needed me, too, that day.

But the detectives come and question. They had to go through every building that was burnt, like through your house, to see if there was any remains of anybody. And then they'd put up a red

Figure 46. Commemorative plaque for Sarah McHarg, near Currency Creek. 15 November, 2013. Photo: Jiayuan Liang.

tape around each building as they went through there. Those detectives really give me the works, because I didn't leave. And I said, 'Look here! I'm still here!' I said, 'When my cows are trying to calve over night time, I'm over the paddock with them. I didn't leave them then, and I wasn't leaving them now.' I said, 'And if it happened again,' I said, 'I wouldn't go!' No, I really copped it from them. But, anyway, like I said: I'm still here; I survived it.

But afterwards, nature wouldn't let me realise that I didn't have anything left. Even nowadays, I go to look for something, and I can't find it. I mean, you had everything. But a few hours later, you couldn't even get a drink of water. Your tanks were all busted, the solder melted in the galvanised ones; the concrete ones – they burst – and things like that. But the part that hurt me that night, I didn't have any food for my dogs! That's what worried me. My brother and sister-in-law lived not far away. They were lucky; their house didn't burn. So I went over there that evening. But then I come back, and I had one little garage there that was left. Of all the buildings, that was left. It didn't burn, and it had a forty-four gallon drum of fuel in it, and that didn't burn. Did you ever? I could never. But I always reckon there was this shrub. You might have heard of the shrub boobialla. That's the one that doesn't burn. The garage had a hedge of that by it, and I reckon that's what saved that.

You'd go down to your house, I went sifting through, 'cause I had all these hundreds of trophies I'd won in photography. Oh, and I had this beautiful collection of pepper and salt shakers. I had over two hundred pairs of pepper and salt shakers. I knew exactly where they were in the corner of the place. I picked up these sheets of iron, and there was one. I had a squirrel, and he had a pepper and salt shaker, one in each arm. Everything was burnt around him: the cupboard, the house, the roof had fell down on him, and he was still sitting there in the ashes – when I shifted the ashes. I could see this orangey coloured thing, and I thought, 'What is that?' And it was him, and he was still sitting there with his pepper and salt shaker things in his arms. And that's when I broke down. I couldn't take it! It really caught up with me, and I really broke down then. I couldn't take it. And I thought, 'Gee, that's given me fresh hope.' There he was, everything else melted around him, and this little squirrel with his pepper and salt shakers. He's coming over to the museum when I've gone. There's a picture of him in the museum out there, now. I said, 'He's got to be taken in. He can go live in the museum when I don't have him.'

It's strange. I was never, ever bitter that I'd lost everything. A lot of people thought: Oh, why should it happen to them? But I just felt so sorry for everyone else that had lost, because I knew what they were going through. That's the way it was. But I have

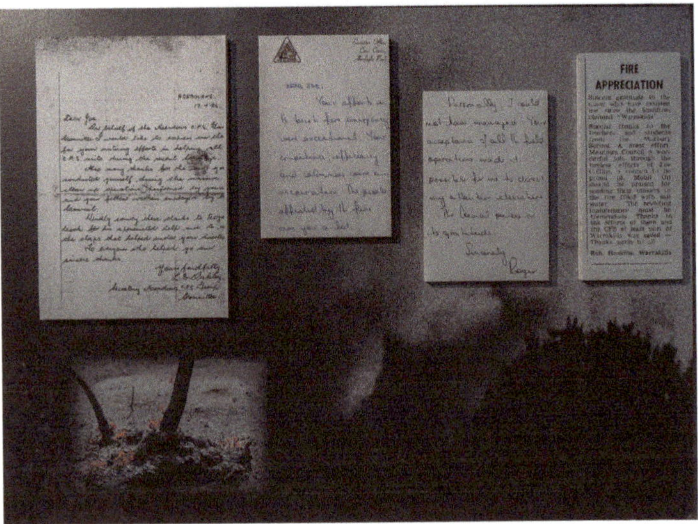


Figure 47. (a) Ash Wednesday bushfires museum display, Prospect Hill Museum, and (b) personal appreciations after Ash Wednesday bushfires. 13 October, 2020. Photos: Jiayuan Liang.

# Joyce Smart

It is heartbreaking to see everything you've ever had all your life just lying there in ashes. I had a collection of salt and pepper shakers that I thought was gone. A few days after the fire as I was sorting through the ashes of my home, I lifted a piece of tin and sitting proudly underneath was a little ceramic squirrel with an acorn on each shoulder - one for salt and one for pepper. It was then that the flood of emotion hit me.

Joyce Smart

47 (c) Joyce Smart's squirrel with pepper and salt shakers, 13 October, 2020. Photo: Jiayuan Liang.

47 (d) Greg and Gail Morrison, Prospect Hill Museum. Photo: Jiayuan Liang.

# Early Homestead Destroyed

"Orange Bank" the home of five generations of the Oakley family over the last 105 years, was one of the victims of the Ash Wednesday fires.

Built by John Oakley in the 1870's, it replaced the original family home of wattle and daub which stood on the same property.

The last members of the family to live here were the late Arch Oakley's son, Malcolm, his wife and two elder daughters. About 16 years ago he moved to Noosa Heads, Queensland, since when it had been rented out.

The fire gave a tragic ending to a homestead which has given shelter to so many members of this well known local family. It was here that the young couple Miss Jane Winifred Gregurke (23) and Mr. Warren John McCourt (24) of Ascot Park, Adelaide met their deaths in heat so intense it buckled steel and twisted stoneware. Yet in the front garden oranges still cling to the tree, albeit cooked, and green grass reaches almost to the front steps.

The ruins of "Orange Bank".

# Strathalbyn Young Libs

**The Strathalbyn Districts Young Liberal Club has decided to celebrate St. Patrick's Day with a dinner at the Terminus Hotel featuring Mr. John Olsen, the Leader of the Opposition, as the keynote speaker.**

The night of 17th March starts off at 7 p.m. and the cost to cover the meal is $11 per person.

If anyone would like to hear the future Premier of South Australia in a relaxed manner and over a good meal, tickets are available from Pat Secker (08) 388 9368 or Trevor McLean (085) 37 0078.

People of all ages are welcome.

Strathalbyn Young Libs are planning a number of fundraising activities over the next three years to raise money for State and Federal elections due at about that time.

Next meeting is on Friday the 15th April and consists of a Dinner / Debate against Norwood Young Liberals.

The topic is "That Marriage Makes the Man".



# Richest Ever Cup for Strathalbyn Trots

**The Minister of Recreation and Sport the Hon. Jack Slater M.P. will be at the Strathalbyn Trotting Track next Sunday March 13th to present the 1983 Oyster Bed Pacing Cup.**

An unprecedented number of nominations for the seven event program will ensure that all races will be of the highest possible standard.

Every person entering the course will receive a voucher to the Oyster Bed Restaurant, Klemzig, entitling them to a free main course meal.

There are six dozen bottles of Orlando Wine to be given away to those people lucky enough to possess a winning numbered racebook.

The Terminus Hotel will make available bottles of wine and beer as prizes in a draw of losing betting tickets which are to be placed in the barrell provided in the bar area.

Mr. David Leak, proprietor of the Oyster Bed Restaurant and now a resident in the Strathalbyn area, has made a significant contribution to the Strathalbyn Trotting Club through his generous sponsorship, which has enabled the club to attract a better and more consistent class of horse to the Strathalbyn track.

The Oyster Bed Pacing Cup is now one of the richest Country Cups in South Australia which could rival the Kapunda and Gawler Cup in the near future.

With all this activity and more, the place to be this Sunday is the Strathalbyn Paceway with racing commencing at 1 p.m.

# The South East Assembly Of The Catholic Church

**The delegates to the South East Regional Assembly of the Catholic Church, express deep sorrow at the tragic loss and suffering of many people who were affected by the Ash Wednesday fires.**

The Assembly assures these people of support in prayer, and urges all men and women of good will, to continue sensitively supporting them. This support will be needed beyond the short term. It will need to persevere.

The Assembly which met last weekend feels that its main aims have been achieved.

Delegates have reviewed the life of faith in their parishes and shared this view.

Delegates have reported and shared the strengths their parishes have, and in this way have learned from each other.

With the help of Archbishop James Gleeson, the chief pastor of the Archdiocese of Adelaide, of which the South East is part, delegates have recognised more deeply the important mission that they ... ioners in the spirit of Faith.

Key points raised in the Assembly include-

- The strengths and resources this region has in its Lay people, Clergy and religious.
- The great extent of involvement by Lay people in the life of the Church today. Lay ministers of the Eucharist were highlighted as being a key development.

**Leadership** - seen mainly as a work of service for people, and exercised through witness to the Gospel of Jesus in our community.

**Communication** - further communication is necessary between parishes in the region and within parishes themselves.

Some frustration was experienced by delegates due to the lack of time to share ...

# Strathalbyn Soccer

by "Offside"

Saturday morning saw the second pre-season practice for the 1983 soccer season.

Matches begin on the 9th of April when practices will transfer to Thursday afternoons from 3.45 p.m. to 5.15 p.m. for Primary teams and Sunday mornings 10 a.m. - 12 noon for the Under 14.

This year there are four teams, Under 8, Under 10 and Open Primary and for the first time an Under 14 team made up of high school boys.

Approximately eight children, (both boys and girls) in each of the under 8 and under 10 teams attended, with 9 in a combined Open Primary and under 14 team.

Practices begin with warm up exercises involving all children, then they separate into each team for skills practice and finish with a scratch match involving all children.

# February Rainfall Recordings

| Township | Yearly Aver. | Totals to end of Jan. | Totals for Feb | Totals to Date | This Time Last Year |
|---|---|---|---|---|---|
| Callington | 376 | 9.8 | 1.6 | 11.4 | 14.8 |
| Langhorne Creek | 392 | 6.6 | 2.4 | 9.0 | 22.8 |
| Milang | 385 | 9.0 | 1.4 | 10.4 | 23.6 |
| Strathalbyn | 495 | 9.3 | 3.0 | 12.3 | 20.4 |
| Finniss | 490 | 9.2 | 5.0 | 14.2 | 28.4 |
| Goolwa | 467 | 7.2 | 2.8 | 10.0 | 33.2 |
| Port Elliot | 506 | 17.0 | 4.7 | 21.7 | 26.2 |
| Victor Harbor | 536 | 9.8 | 3.8 | 13.6 | 22.8 |
| Yankalilla | 581 | 5.0 | 5.6 | 10.6 | 23.0 |
| Myponga | 765 | 6.2 | 3.2 | 9.4 | 24.0 |
| Aldinga | 502 | 5.4 | 5.0 | 10.4 | 34.2 |
| Macclesfield | 747 | 18.0 | 2.0 | 20.0 | 26.0 |
| Echunga | 814 | 19.4 | Nil | 19.4 | 31.0 |
| Bridgewater | 1049 | 34.3 | 1.1 | 35.4 | 37.4 |



Figure 48. Early Homestead Destroyed, *Southern Argus*, Thursday 24 February 1983, p. 9.

Figure 49. The property Orangebank today. 15 November, 2020. Photo: Jiayuan Liang.

coped. It's funny, on the thirtieth anniversary last year, I got calls from channel two and all. They come out and interviewed me. It brought it all back as though the time after that had never happened. It's something you can never forget all your life. But, no, I'm not bitter that it happened. It happened. I mean, it happens to so many around here. I think there were sixteen houses burnt.

Unfortunately, there was a young couple burnt in one down at Blackfellows Creek. They weren't locals. They were there looking after the property for a young lass that had gone on her honeymoon. Those two got burnt to death. They were young city people; they didn't realise what would happen. They had a dog tied up outside on a big long – thank goodness it was a rope. That dog, he'd been caught alight, because part of him was burnt. But his rope had burnt through and next day they found him. He had enough sense, he'd gone and got in a dam. He stood in the dam and put himself out. He was still alive, you know. And yet, the young couple, they were burnt to death and that was dreadful.

But a day like that, there could have been dozens of people. Everybody – nearly everybody – cleared out and went to the Meadows oval. They didn't stay. But, like I said, I wasn't going. I stayed. But I'm still here to tell the story.

We lost so much. We lost the CWA Hall – that was burnt. But then Wollongong donated all that money to build the community centre over there across the road, which was a wonderful thing. The war memorial hall, all the doors were burnt off of that. But the hall wasn't burnt, thank goodness, only the woodwork and that. Oh, and of course the old school – that all got burnt, the schoolhouse up on the hill.

And, of course, nature – the trees, all the trees. After a few weeks, all the leaves went brown – they all went brown – then all dropped off. There wasn't a green thing anywhere. Everything was black. Oh, it was terrible. And then we got a big rain about three weeks after. The trees all started to shoot with all this beautiful new shoots, especially our stringy barks. Some of them, like the pink gums and that, didn't survive. And of course pines don't, because it just boils all the resin. They'd never shoot. That was a business for the pine industry. They lost thousands. They were carting the logs right down to Mount Gambier, putting them in the lakes there to try to keep. Because as you know, pine will not keep for long. Then it grew this blue mould in it when it was in the lakes down there. My brother, he was a pine cutter. He was cutting all these burnt pines. Oh, that was a terrible business, that was. And it was only from here to the oak tree away from my property where they were burning, like I said, over a hundred feet high.

The buildings out here, we lost so much out there in the outbuildings. There was big horse stables – oh, beautiful

Figure 50. Greg Morrison, Prospect Hill Museum. 15 November, 2020. Photo: Jiayuan Liang.

buildings, some of those – they all got burnt. And the two-storied one out there now where the Ash Wednesday display is. That's been built to the same as it was before. That one's been replaced. But, oh, it was dreadful. When it first happened, you'd never think Prospect Hill could ever build up again as quick as it did. We've got an Ash Wednesday display out the back. It tells the history of what did happen. We got a grant to do that. Otherwise, we couldn't have done that. I get so many children that come here and you take them out there and you show them just what can happen, 'cause they weren't born yet. That was thirty-one years ago. Most them have never, ever seen such a frightening thing to know what a fire can really do, especially from the city and that. They'd have no idea. They'd see pictures on TV, I know, but it's amazing the emotions that people have when they go out there, and they read the things and see them. Yes, it affects them of all different ages, that's for sure.

Following Ash Wednesday, more efforts have been put into protecting and preserving the heritage of Prospect Hill. I reckon we should appreciate what we've got more now than ever. What we have got left, it could have all been gone. If this property here were burnt, just imagine. Because none of this stuff can ever be replaced. It all dates back to 1872, so that's a long time.

The CFS is wonderful. They've got such better equipment and that nowadays. We couldn't survive without the CFS, that's for sure. They're quite a strong group. They have to have a full crew before they're allowed to go out on a fire. I don't know, I suppose there'd be, probably twelve, fifteen of them, I suppose. Some girls as well, not only the men. But they're always on call, I mean twenty-four hours a day. No, the place wouldn't exist without them. The trouble is, a lot of them, like I said, those young men, they've got to work in the city. And the CFS is not only fires. They have to attend to accidents and that. They've got to go when there's a car accident, 'cause there's usually a fire. And when there's trees down over the road through the night, it's the CFS. It's not the Council people that's doing it. The CFS are the ones out cutting all the trees and that off the roads. Oh, they're wonderful, they really are.

But the Council's very good to us at the museum because they provide somebody to keep all the grass and everything cut around all the buildings. That's a big help. That's cut regularly and kept. And we have working bees around here trying to keep the rubbish and that down.

We've got sprinklers on the buildings here, the community centre and the museum – this building – was set up with sprinklers. There's a motor, like an auxiliary motor, up there that can be started. And the big tank up there with all the water. So if there's a fire, somebody has to be responsible to start the sprinklers and try and save this building anyway. But the outbuildings haven't got anything like that. The main thing is to try to keep the high grass down in the summertime. That's one of the most important things, I think. But we haven't got anywhere where we can sort of store stuff. If there is a fire coming, it's just got to be protected where it is.

In the future I'm hoping the museum is going to be kept the way it is, that's for sure. It's something so precious that must always be here. I hope to goodness that it will always be here. But we never know, do we? We don't know what's going to happen. Anything can happen. But I hope that it'll be here in a hundred years' time for the young, for the generations, so that they can enjoy it and get as much pleasure out of it as we do today. Because people come in here and they just step back in time. They don't want to see it all modern and all like that. They want to see how the people used to be. When we was first starting it as a museum, we wanted it to be a living memorial to the pioneering families, because it shows you how they lived, and the things they used to have to use and all of that. And that's the way it must be kept. It must never be changed to lose that wonderful feeling. Because they come in here and they just stand and look, and they say, 'Oh, great-grandma used to have that!' It's wonderful to see the people, how they can go. I always say, you can step back in time when you come in here. And if you just stand here in the peace and the quiet, you can imagine the way they'd lived in those days. There wasn't that hustle and bustle. They were all going at a slower pace in those days. And what a difference it made.

We were so pleased to have what we have got left. It must be looked after, that's for sure. For generations, because how awful it would be if these things wasn't here for us to see. I always think if anybody destroyed anything, what a dreadful thing to take it away so generations can't see what we could have had the pleasure of seeing. And the children, they can't believe it. 'Oh, where was their fridge?' And 'where was something else?' The little kids, they can't believe it. And where they used to have to make candles because they didn't have a light at night. Things like that. I'm sure that having this has helped Prospect Hill recover from the bushfire. It helped me. Being a hoarder, and a sentimentalist, I had nothing of my stuff left: anything that I'd ever had from when I was a child. I was only four and eleven months when my father died suddenly. The things that had been given me before, I lost all of those things. I never had anything old or anything that Mum had given me. To be able to come over here and to live amongst the old things, it helped me a lot. It certainly did. It still does. Even if it is a struggle, it's the most important part of my life.

I don't know what will happen in the future. I can't expect newcomers to have the passion that I've got for Prospect Hill. You can't expect that. People that have been here for a few years, it doesn't mean the same to them. But there's always got to be somebody that really wants to keep it going. It's got to be kept going. We've got something so precious. There's so many places, what they'd give to have something like we've got. It's something so precious, what Keith Griggs left us. This museum, what a wonderful thing to have left for a community.

There's a lot of the people, though, some that live in the community, that have never been in here. And yet they come from overseas. I get these letters and cards they send back to me after they'd been here. It's just wonderful! And another thing, being here, and meeting people from all over the world, I get so much out of it. I know people from all the different countries – it's amazing. You just meet so many lovely people. And all the old-fashioned car clubs that come Sunday. They come with all their old motorcars they have, right back to the early 1900s and that. Oh, it's wonderful. I put a lot of time in here, but I get a lot out of it. Pleasure, that's for sure. But I've got friends all over. I can be right away somewhere and somebody will say, 'Oh, hello! You come from the Prospect Hill Museum, don't you?' Oh, it's wonderful. Before Keith passed away, he used to call to Pat and I, 'Hey, you blokes! You got to look after that place when I'm gone!'. And I said to Keith, not long before he passed away, 'Keith, I'll do it for as long as I can.' And the last eighteen years, I've missed one Sunday. I had to go away to a ninetieth birthday party and I felt terrible! They was all there eating their cream cakes and all. And I thought, 'Heavens! It's time to open the museum!' No, it's part of my life.

I always say: Prospect Hill – it's the best place on earth. Keith Griggs used to say, 'If Prospect Hill means as much to you as it means to me, there will always be a Prospect Hill.' So there will always be a Prospect Hill.

12 March 2014

Figure 51. Prospect Hill Community Association Meeting, 13 October, 2020.
Photo: Jiayuan Liang.

# Afterword

My mind often turns to the earliest settlers at Prospect Hill. These pioneers were mostly born on the other side of the world but they saw something in the area to be known as Prospect Hill that would keep them here for multiple generations. From the first timber, bark and grass 'huts' that provided some sort of shelter to the cob wall construction of the Griggs home that now serves as the museum, there was a determination to strive for permanency, whatever the consequences and outcomes. When these pioneers built their homesteads they created succession plans for their families. They were building in the moment, but their vision was long-term.

So much has come and gone. We have little knowledge of Aboriginal use of the lands around us. Also, few of the stories from early settlement have been told. However, the opportunity to contribute to a permanent record of over 100 years of life in this little patch of the Southern Mount Lofty Ranges could not be missed. The histories contained in this book are a permanent record available for those with no more than a general interest through to descendants, relatives and kin folk who may crave an insight into the lives of those who came before them. This book will fill a lot of gaps that are important to people who are connected to Prospect Hill.

The very existence of Prospect Hill was never so threatened as it was on Ash Wednesday in 1983. Terrible things happened on that day, but miracles also happened so not all was lost. This is a resilient community with a strong impetus to rebuild. For example, the home my family lives in rose from the ashes of the Prospect Hill School, proof of an attainment of permanency regardless of the challenges. Cultural heritage has been an important anchor in the rebuilding process.

Even today, we live with the threat of bushfires. However, it is unlikely that we would have another Ash Wednesday as the load was greatly reduced. At the time of the Ash Wednesday bushfire a tunnel of pines existed along Morris Road. Their branches joined overhead forming a tunnel. Those pines were destroyed on Ash Wednesday. Since then, we have been much more aware of the risk and more diligent about controlling the growth. We are alert, but not alarmed.

Thank you to all who are responsible for this publication. Over time it will be viewed as a small but very valuable contribution to the memories of a burned village.

Greg Morrison
President, Prospect Hill Community Association
10th November, 2020

Wakefield Press is an independent publishing and distribution company based in Adelaide, South Australia. We love good stories and publish beautiful books. To see our full range of books, please visit our website at www.wakefieldpress.com.au where all titles are available for purchase. To keep up with our latest releases, news and events, subscribe to our monthly newsletter.

Find us!

Facebook: www.facebook.com/wakefield.press
Twitter: www.twitter.com/wakefieldpress
Instagram: www.instagram.com/wakefieldpress

Printed in Australia
AUHW011519060521
345189AU00005B/5

9 781743 058350